Mr. Justice Rehnquist, Judicial Activist

THE EARLY YEARS

Mr. Justice Rehnquist, Judicial Activist

THE EARLY YEARS

Donald E. Boles

Iowa State University Press
AMES

Donald E. Boles is Professor of Political Science at Iowa State University.

© 1987 Iowa State University Press, Ames, Iowa 50010

Composed by Iowa State University Press
Printed in the United States of America

First edition, 1987

Library of Congress Cataloging-in-Publication Data

Boles, Donald E. (Donald Edward), 1926–
    Mr. Justice Rehnquist, judicial activist: the early years

    Bibliography: p.
    Includes index.
    1. Rehnquist, William H., 1924- . 2. Judges—United States—Selection and appointment. 3. United States. Supreme Court. 4. Political questions and judicial power—United States. 5. Civil rights—United States. I. Title. II. Title: Mister Justice Rehnquist, judicial activist.
KF8745.R44B65   1987   347.73′2634   87-3295
ISBN 0-8138-1116-3   347.3073534

For Fran

and her unceasing endeavor to square the rounders

Contents

Preface, ix

1   Personal and Intellectual Origins, 3

2   Political Theories and Labels, 19

3   Media Views on the Rehnquist Philosophy, 35

4   Mr. Justice Rehnquist and Civil Liberties, 55

5   Early Racial Views, 75

6   More Controversy over Race, Theory, and Procedure, 97

7   The End of the Beginning, 115

Notes, 135

Index, 143

Preface

THIS is the first of what is planned to be a several-volume study of Chief Justice William H. Rehnquist. I will place particular emphasis on his views on civil liberties and his attitudes toward the judicial process and governmental authority in relation to the individual. In this volume, that portion of his life and thought are reviewed that cover the period before and up to the point he assumed his duties as an associate justice of the Supreme Court. In a sense it takes Mr. Rehnquist at his word when he says that he believes his views on the role of government and the courts in relation to individual rights have changed very little since he moved to the bench. If this is true, it would seem especially important to look carefully at the early instances and manner in which he revealed his intellectual outlook on these subjects.

It is probably true that it is more important to observe the way a person acts rather than the way he talks if one hopes to obtain an accurate portrait of the individual. In the case of Chief Justice Rehnquist, however, there is an almost amazing consistency between the man's words before arriving on the Court and his deeds as reflected in his later written opinions and other public statements.

As this is written, Rehnquist is serving his first months in his new role as Chief Justice of the United States. He attained this position only after numerous acrimonious Senate confirmation hearings and after he had received more votes against his confirmation than any other justice who had won an appointment to the Court. Because of the "Iran-gate" controversy, some observers see the influence and power of President Reagan and the right-wing ideologues waning. What effect this may have on Rehnquist's influence among his brethren on the Court and on his personal approach to judicial decision making will be interesting to observe.

If past behavior is any indication of future trends, however, it should be remembered that the new chief justice has never been one to trim his sails in order to ride easily with the winds of public opinion. After all, his reply when asked what qualities a president should look for when selecting a justice of the Supreme Court was, "You have to be able to stand on your own two feet . . . Not being bamboozled by current trendy ideas . . . Not easily conned . . . Not awash in current trends of public opinion."[1]

It will be interesting to observe whether the added responsibility and visibility of a chief justice will in any way alter Rehnquist's consistent intellectual and jurisprudential approach when he finds himself in the position of forging the Court that will carry his name. Will the compromise typically necessary to build a majority opinion affect the fixed stars in his firmament of values, or will the addition of the recently appointed and like-minded Judge Antonin Scalia (and possibly others of a similar viewpoint who might soon fill vacancies yet unannounced) make it unnecessary for him to engage in the moderating role of coalition builder? These are questions certain to intrigue the minds of Court-watchers for the next few years.

In this study I have made every attempt to present Rehnquist's views and actions in as accurate a fashion as the human psyche permits. In a similar fashion, I have tried to present a representative cross section of the criticism that has surfaced over his many controversial stands. There is, indeed, much to be said for the old saw that one can judge a man by the enemies he makes. On the other hand, it would be disingenuous of me (to use a term frequently applied to Chief Justice Rehnquist's opinions by critical legal scholars) to imply in any way that I find much logical attraction or policy appeal in the Rehnquist approach to constitutional history, jurisprudence, or the relationship between government and the individual.

I wish to thank the Department of Political Science of Iowa State University for its support of this study and also to express my appreciation to Chen-Feng Shih and Man Hyung Cho, who served as my research assistants during its preparation. Any errors found here are, of course, my own.

Mr. Justice Rehnquist, Judicial Activist

THE EARLY YEARS

1
Personal and Intellectual Origins

THINGS were a bit testy in the Nixon White House those golden mid-October days in 1971. The vacancies left on the Supreme Court by the retirement of Justices Hugo L. Black and John M. Harlan would normally have brought joy to the heart of President Nixon and his lieutenants, intent as they were on remaking the Court in their own ideological image. They were, however, still smarting from the wounds suffered in two defeats a year before. Then, to fill one vacancy on the Court, they had attempted in vain to sell two appointees, Judges Clement F. Haynsworth of South Carolina and G. Harrold Carswell of Florida, to an outraged Congress and a bemused public. That position had finally been filled through the confirmation of Justice Harry A. Blackmun of Minnesota.

Now, to make matters worse, a plan they had devised to return at least a semblance of respectability to the judicial nominating process had backfired on them. The key to their strategy was the public announcement on 23 July 1970 by Attorney General John N. Mitchell that he would not refer a potential nominee to the president without first checking his or her legal qualifications with the American Bar Association's Committee on the Federal Judiciary. It seemed a relatively safe and innocuous proceeding because, after all, the ABA committee had been rating Supreme Court nominees as

3

far back as the Eisenhower years without ever finding one who was not qualified.

One can appreciate the Nixon team's horror, then, when—after weeks of apparently careful search for and scrutiny of potential candidates, with attendant fanfare about the need for top-quality people and a well-announced sensitivity to the consideration of women as well as ideologically compatible candidates for the post—the ABA committee, in a precedent-shattering move on 20 October 1971, found both of the administration's candidates to be "Not Qualified" for the empty seats of Black and Harlan. The embarrassment of the White House was not diminished by the fact that the press was widely noting that Mildred L. Lillie of Los Angeles and Herschel H. Friday, a Little Rock, Arkansas, lawyer, were in line to be named to the Supreme Court. Bitter criticism of the rumored choices followed immediately. Moreover, the committee's vote of 11 to 1 in finding Mrs. Lillie to be "Not Qualified" was not even close. Its 6-to-6 vote in finding Mr. Friday "Not Qualified" might at best be considered damning with faint praise so far as the Senate and the American Bar were concerned.

In this light, perhaps President Nixon's pique could be the excuse for his privately growling to his staff his off-color thoughts involving the use of a four-letter word to describe what in his judgment should be done to the American Bar Association.[1] The evening following the announcement of the committee's vote, Attorney General Mitchell terminated the administration's arrangement with the ABA, charging that there had been unauthorized disclosures—news leaks—of the committee's deliberations.

Moments before the Mitchell statement, President Nixon named William Rehnquist and Lewis Powell to the Supreme Court of the United States. White House press secretary Ronald L. Ziegler later told reporters that the names of the nominees had not been submitted to the ABA because Mr. Nixon "doubted the confidentiality of the process."[2] When Ziegler was asked about the role of the ABA in the appointments, he said he was not going to discuss the consultations of the attorney general with the ABA. In the days just preceding these appointments, the press secretary had attempted to put some space between the president and Mr. Mitchell. He emphasized that it was the attorney general, not the president, who was consulting with the ABA. "The President has decided to proceed," Ziegler said. "The Senate has a responsibility to give its advice and consent. The Constitution does not require the consent of the ABA."[3]

The major question in the mind of even the most casual observer of this process was, Why did Mr. Nixon initially prefer less distinguished choices for the Court? A good argument can be made that in planning the appointments the administration had attempted to accomplish too many political goals that were at best incidental to the goal of maintaining a strong Supreme Court. Certainly there seems to have been excessive concentration on such raw political considerations as appointing a woman, pleasing segregationist sentiment in the South, and cementing a law-and-order philosophy into the Court by naming conservatives who were relatively young. But time was to show that most of these goals would be accomplished by the subsequent appointment of William Rehnquist.

Interestingly enough, Rehnquist himself had earlier seen the pitfalls involved in the Nixon nominating process. When in September 1971 he had been asked whether he had any chance of landing one of the posts on the Court, he replied with a smile, "None at all, because I'm not from the South, I'm not a woman, and I'm not mediocre."[4]

Some of Rehnquist's views on women and the Equal Rights Amendment (ERA) had been formulated one year earlier in a memo sent to the White House at the request of the legal counsel to the president, Leonard Garment, to balance the arguments presented by a female attorney in Rehnquist's Office of Legal Counsel within the Justice Department. In the memorandum Mr. Rehnquist said that the proposed Equal Rights Amendment would "virtually abolish all legal distinctions between men and women" and "hasten the dissolution of the family."[5] "I cannot help thinking," the Rehnquist memo said, that there is within the women's movement "a virtually fanatical desire to obscure not only legal differentiation between men and women, but insofar as possible, physical distinctions between the sexes." Mr. Rehnquist also said in the memo that under state laws, "the domicile of a married woman has been that of her husband, and if her husband decides to move from Boston to Chicago in order to take a different job, the wife is legally obligated to accompany him (as well as being obligated by virtue of traditional marriage vows and most religious teaching)." The ERA, he explained, "would leave both parties with the power to decide this question—with a result that could indeed, to paraphrase a famous English author, turn 'holy wedlock' into 'holy deadlock.' "

As Rehnquist stated in his memo, the ERA's language was so vague that it could lead the courts to abolish many of the preferences traditionally accorded women. "It is highly dubious, in my mind," he wrote, "whether a great majority of American women, to say nothing of American men, if they knew that this were the main thrust of the 'equal rights amendment,' would support it." "Do a majority of women," he asked, "wish to see their preferential treatment under the Social Security Act taken away? Do a majority of women wish to be deprived of special protection in hazardous occupations? Do a majority of women wish to be eligible for the military draft?" "Put in broader terms," he said, "do a majority of women really wish to have the only distinction between themselves and men be the preservation of separate rest rooms in public buildings?" He went on to say that "the results appear almost certain to have an adverse effect on the family unit as we have known it."

What the Equal Rights Amendment actually said was: "Equality of rights under the law shall not be denied or abridged by the United States or by any state on account of sex." The Nixon administration later endorsed the ERA, which failed in 1982 after winning approval from thirty-five states, three fewer than needed for ratification.

When the Rehnquist memo finally surfaced publicly in the 1986 debate over his confirmation as chief justice, it brought an immediate and angry reaction from a variety of women's groups. According to an Associated Press story carried in the *Des Moines Register* on 10 September 1986, Judith Lichtman, executive director of the Women's Legal Defense Fund, said upon learning the contents of the memo that it reflects an "extreme position" and a "deep-seated animosity to women's basic rights as partners in the family." Rehnquist, she said, "has an archaic notion of the family. In his view, men are masters of the house, and Rehnquist fears that an Equal Rights Amendment would undermine a man's right to determine all decisions in the house." Eleanor Smeal, president of the National Organization for Women, was quoted in the same story as calling the Rehnquist memo the "most reactionary argument I've seen against women in a long time."

Judy Mann, in her 12 September 1986 column in the *Washington Post,* noted that "Justice Rehnquist's efforts to preserve traditional family values (read: barefoot, pregnant and in the kitchen) have until quite recently been hidden from history." With the appearance of the ERA memo, Mann notes, it now appears that Justice Rehnquist was "among the first to recognize that the Equal Rights Amendment was, in fact, part of a plot hatched by a bunch of fanatical women who wanted to obscure not only legal but also physical differences between men and women." "Why," she wonders, "Gloria Steinem would want to look like a man, I do not know, but she was an active conspirator in this plot, so it must be her goal."

In a 15 September 1986 editorial entitled, "Just Say No on Rehnquist," the *Des Moines Register* advised, "If the senators need more evidence of Rehnquist's all-male WASPish perspective, consider the just-uncovered memo." There is, the paper said, "no need to belabor the implications of this memo, for it merely confirms what opponents of Rehnquist have been saying all along: that his mind seems stuck in 1950." Rehnquist, the paper went on, "is not only sadly out of touch with contemporary American values but with the values embodied in the Constitution." The paper conceded

7

that there was little chance that the Republican-controlled Senate would reject the appointment, but it concluded, "That may be good politics, but it is not statesmanship, because it will result in a chief justice whose veracity, integrity, ethical standards, and hence, judgment will always be open to question."

Ironically, in his speech nominating Powell and Rehnquist, the president stressed the fact that both men met his "standard of excellence to an exceptional degree." He explained that both were honor graduates of their law schools and that Powell had received "every honor of the legal profession." He described Rehnquist as the government's chief interpreter of the Constitution and statutes and "one of the finest legal minds in the whole nation today."

In his speech, the president, while paying tribute to Justices Black and Harlan as "great judges," went on to express his own philosophy and that of his nominees. Mr. Nixon said that "As a judicial conservative, I believe some court decisions have gone too far in weakening the peace forces against the criminal forces of our society." He said that he wished to see the balance redressed and that the "peace forces must not be deprived of the tools needed to protect society against criminals." This end could be accomplished with his two appointees, he explained, since both were legal conservatives. According to the 22 October 1971 *Washington Post,* the president went on to say that it was his "firm conviction" that Powell and Rehnquist would "earn the same respect" that the other two Nixon appointees, Warren E. Burger and Harry Blackmun, had won and that "as guardians of our Constitution they will dedicate their lives to the great goal of building respect for law and order and justice throughout this great land of ours."

Despite his warm words of praise for Mr. Rehnquist's ability and the suggestion of a close working relationship with him, the *Washington Post* reported that three months before he "proudly named Rehnquist to the Supreme Court," President Nixon "denounced his assistant attorney general as part of a 'group of clowns' fumbling an investigation of

8

national security leaks." The transcript of a taped 24 July 1971 White House meeting quotes Mr. Nixon as complaining to domestic advisor John D. Ehrlichman: "Nobody follows up on a God damn thing. You remember the meeting we had when I told that group of clowns we had around here. Renchburg and that group. What's his name?" "Rehnquist," Ehrlichman said. "Yeah. Rehnquist," Mr. Nixon said, finally getting it right.[6]

In announcing the two Supreme Court appointments on 21 October 1971, Mr. Nixon told a national television audience, "Lewis Powell, William Rehnquist. Those are names you will remember, because they will add distinction and excellence in the highest degree to the Supreme Court of the United States."

One thing was clear, the name William Hubbs Rehnquist was not a household word those first days in the autumn of 1971. Furthermore, the portrait that began to emerge in the period leading up to the Senate hearings on his confirmation clearly suggested that this was not a man to fit Senator Roman Hruska's plaintive argument that the mediocre also should have some representation on the Supreme Court. Hruska's remarks followed earlier attacks on Judge G. Harrold Carswell on the grounds that he was at best mediocre. As the Republican senator so memorably put it, "even if he [Carswell] was mediocre, there are a lot of mediocre judges and people and lawyers. They are entitled to a little representation, aren't they, and a little chance? We can't have all Brandeises and Cardozos and Frankfurters and stuff like that."[7]

William Rehnquist was mediocre neither in his academic accomplishments nor in the emotions he stirred in those who supported or opposed his views, both prior to and after taking a job with the Justice Department. History was to demonstrate that the hotly divided reactions to his legal positions and ideology were to grow even more pronounced once he assumed his post on the Supreme Court.

According to Ken W. Clawson, writing in the *Washington Post* the day after his nomination, Rehnquist "looks like an

over-age college sophomore, and his low-key image contributed to the belief in some spheres of the administration that
he came out of nowhere to land the nomination, but the image is deceiving."[8] Clawson went on to point out that
Rehnquist had emerged as the leading administration official
working to make fundamental changes in the criminal justice system, that as the president's lawyer Rehnquist had
approved the constitutionality of the Philadelphia plan for
hiring minority members in the construction trades (a plan
later upheld by the Supreme Court), and that he had made
the technical changes in the presidential order suspending
the Davis-Bacon Act, which set standards for construction
wages.

From the first, it was recognized that Rehnquist was a
political conservative—a Goldwater Republican—but according to Clawson's early story, his associates in the Justice Department, many of them career employees who had been
there since before the Republicans had taken over, admired
"his ability to pull back from a close legal call and summarize
both sides of the issue." One career aide, Mary Lawton, told
Clawson, "The law comes first with [Rehnquist], and the law
can turn him around on an issue." Another associate said,
"When he came to Washington, he had a strong state's rights
orientation. But on specific issues he shows a human, com-
passionate vein that modifies his views. Now, I'd say he's a
case by case man, and I agree the law can and does turn him
around."[9]

In a telephone interview on the night he was nominated
by Mr. Nixon, Rehnquist told Clawson that he had "grown
and his outlook ha[d] broadened since [being] recruited for
the Justice Department" in 1969. "Well, it's one thing to deal
with a client or a group of clients on a single issue, and it's
quite another to discuss law that affects the whole country,"
Rehnquist said. "I don't see how a person could fail to
broaden his horizons in my job." He then added that he did
not plan to comment further until after his Senate confirmation. As he put it, "You can't be shot for what you didn't
say."[10]

10

Initial reactions from the legislative branch, while indicating that few legislators knew much about Rehnquist, were generally favorable. Senate Judiciary Committee chairman James O. Eastland (D-Miss.) said Rehnquist was a "lawyer's lawyer and would make an outstanding justice." Representative Emanuel Celler (D-N.Y.), a strong civil rights supporter, called the appointment "on the whole, good." He said that Rehnquist was "presentable, very erudite, he will grow with the job." Representative Paul N. McCloskey, Jr. (R-Calif.), said, "I know Bill Rehnquist, we were at Stanford Law School together. Although he has conservative views, he has an excellent legal mind and will be a welcome addition to the Supreme Court." On the other hand, a sour comment came from New York mayor John V. Lindsay, who said, "The President's Supreme Court nominees are a disappointment." He went on to call Rehnquist "undistinguished."[11]

Senator Edmund Muskie (D-Maine), appearing on the CBS television program "Face the Nation," said that the Senate should inquire into Rehnquist's views on mass arrests, First Amendment rights, and other controversial issues with which the nominee had been involved. Muskie said he was reserving judgment, but added, "I could find other nominations that would please me more."[12]

Nonetheless, by the time of the confirmation hearings a sharp division on the candidate had begun to emerge. The dispute did not center on Rehnquist's legal credentials, which all sides agreed were of the highest quality. The strident differences of opinion concerned his judicial philosophy and what was seen by some as his rigid ideological and doctrinaire right-wing view of issues in constitutional law. The rancorous nature of the dispute spilled over from the hearings of the Senate Judiciary Committee into an emotion-packed debate on the floor of the Senate.

The American Civil Liberties Union broke a fifty-two-year tradition of never opposing a nominee for public office and called publicly for Rehnquist's defeat as "a dedicated opponent of individual civil liberties."[13] Rehnquist was also called "another Carswell, only worse," a "right-wing zealot," and a "racist."[14] On the other hand, Senator Barry Goldwater lavishly praised him in a guest column in the *New York Times* as "a man of the highest personal integrity."[15] Kevin Phillips, the conservative syndicated columnist, called him a "shy, intellectual, . . . public servant . . . blessed with honesty and straightforwardness."[16] James J. Kilpatrick, in his syndicated column, said Rehnquist was "superlatively qualified for service on the Court."[17] Thus, while those who knew something of Rehnquist's beliefs, values, and ideology were starkly divided between admiration and loathing, the general public might well be excused for asking, in the vernacular of the day, "Who is that guy?"

Fourteen years after his nomination to the Court, Justice Rehnquist, in a rare and lengthy interview, professed not to know the origins of his conservatism. "It may have something to do with my childhood," he said sarcastically. As John A. Jenkins, who was conducting the interview for the *New York Times*, interpreted the remark, "it was a defensive jibe at any who might comb his past seeking insight to the present." But as Jenkins saw it, "The clues are there."[18]

William Rehnquist and his sister, Jean, had been raised in Shorewood, Wisconsin, an affluent suburb of Milwaukee. Their tan brick home, however, contrasted sharply with the mansions bordering on Lake Michigan. His father, a second-generation American of Swedish parents, had never attended college and was a wholesale paper salesman. His mother was a housewife and was very active in civic affairs. She was especially proud of her University of Wisconsin degree and her fluency in five foreign languages. Additionally, she earned money as a free-lance translator for local companies.

According to his interview with the *New York Times*, dinner in the Rehnquist household was a time for spirited political discussion, and the children learned respect for the Republican views of Alf Landon, Wendell Willkie, Herbert Hoover, and Robert A. Taft. In the all-white Shorewood High School, Rehnquist became feature editor of the school paper

12

and used his forum on the editorial page to make trenchant observations such as, "the recent windy weather may not have been due entirely to weather conditions. Some of the self-styled news 'interpreters' have been doing a little too much spouting of their own. There is no fault to be found with straight news broadcasts; they perform a valuable public service. But thorns to the 'commentators,' the overly dramatic Gabriel Heatter, the pompous H. V. Kaltenborn, and Walter Winchell with his corps of tattlers."[19]

Following the bombing of Pearl Harbor, Rehnquist showed that spark of desire for active participation in public affairs that was to characterize his later life. He volunteered to be a civil-defense officer in his neighborhood and was given responsibility for a network of block captains who were to report to the local police chief any crimes, draft dodging, or, according to his school paper, "subversive activities which might lead to the sabotaging of our national unity."[20] In a state where there had been an active and vocal German-American Bund prior to the outbreak of hostilities, this could have been a more interesting job than young Bill Rehnquist had bargained for. But the record is devoid of his participation in any cloak-and-dagger derring-do.

On graduating from high school, Rehnquist won a scholarship to Kenyon College in Ohio. He only spent one year there (which in itself was quite a feat, given the inclusive quality of the World War II draft) before joining the Army Air Corps as a weather observer in 1943. By the time he was sent to North Africa, hostilities had ended there, but he served in a variety of roles in Cairo, Tunis, Tripoli, and Casablanca. His duty in North Africa was to have a significant impact on his future, however. One thing he learned was that he did not want to suffer through any more of the frigid winters typical of Wisconsin and the Upper Midwest. "I wanted to find someplace like North Africa to go to school," he recalled in his *New York Times* interview.

Bolstered by a federal assistance program called the G.I. Bill, he enrolled at Stanford, in Palo Alto, California. There he majored in political science and graduated Phi Beta Kappa in

13

1948. When his benefits under the G.I. Bill ended, he ran the breakfast program in the university dining hall. "I had so many other part-time jobs, I can't remember them all," he recalls.[21]

In the next two years he received master's degrees from Stanford and Harvard in political science and then returned to Stanford to enter law school. He graduated first in his class in 1952 and with such impressive credentials that he was given a Supreme Court clerkship with Associate Justice Robert H. Jackson, one of the most elegant literary craftsmen ever to sit on the Court.

In his *New York Times* interview he pondered the source of his philosophy, views, and outlook. "How do you get your views?" he mused. "I don't think anybody has any idea. Obviously, there was a long part of my life when I was in high school and in the Army that I just simply didn't give any thought to those things. But I can remember arguments we would get in as law clerks in the early fifties. And I don't know that my views have changed much from that time."

In 1985 he was asked if he considered himself a "partisan." After pondering the question briefly, he replied, "In this sense: I have written opinions and joined opinions that have said that the Fourth Amendment should be construed in this way. I've written opinions and joined opinions that say the establishment clause of the Constitution should be construed in this way. Now, I've thought those things through. I think those opinions are right. And I want to see that version of the law applied when the case comes up. If that makes me a partisan, certainly I'm a partisan. But I don't think that distinguishes me from most of my colleagues."

Jenkins observed that Rehnquist, in breaking his silence, emerged by his statements as a justice who is directed in opinions not so much by *stare decisis* (the doctrine that prior decisions should be followed) as by an "inner compass that almost unfailingly evolved from a moral vision developed long ago." This appears to be essentially what Professor David Shapiro was noting eight years earlier in his brilliant article in the *Harvard Law Review* assessing Rehnquist's first five years on the Court. In analyzing Rehnquist's votes in hundreds of cases, Shapiro concluded that the justice was guided by three basic propositions: (1) Conflicts between the individual and the government should be resolved against the individual, (2) Conflicts between state and federal authority should be resolved in favor of the states, and (3) Questions of the exercise of the jurisdiction of the federal courts should be resolved against such exercise. In his discussion with Jenkins, Justice Rehnquist came at his jurisprudential views from a slightly different direction. "If you think of a judicial conservative as one who generally inclines against broad interpretations of constitutional provisions," he reflected, "I think I am a judicial conservative."[22]

Others, however, have argued that Rehnquist is not a judicial conservative but is instead a judicial activist. Professor Owen Fiss, of the Yale Law School, and Charles Krauthammer, senior editor of *The New Republic*, argued in a 1982 article that this activism was demonstrated in the substance of Rehnquist's beliefs: "Rehnquist has a constitutional program for the nation: he wants to free the states from the restrictions of the national Constitution, particularly those emanating from the Civil War Amendments and the Bill of Rights. His ideal is state autonomy." They note that he has denounced the incorporation doctrine, which has applied the Bill of Rights guarantees to state action in many areas, such as religion and speech. In short, according to these authors, "The states are to be held to an indeterminate lesser standard" if Justice Rehnquist's views prevail.[23]

Fiss and Krauthammer also provide an additional observation in this connection. "Rehnquist's championing of state autonomy," as they see it, "may make him a hero to conservatives, but that acclaim would be ill-deserved. He is no conservative, as that term is ordinarily understood in the law, but rather a revisionist of a particular ideological bent. He repudiates precedents; he shows no deference to the legislative branch; and he is unable to ground state autonomy in any textual provision of the Constitution." As they see it, "he eschews what he calls 'literalism' and speaks instead of the 'implicit ordering of relationships within the federal system' and the 'tacit postulates yielded by that ordering.' "[24]

"I'm a strong believer in pluralism," Justice Rehnquist told Jenkins. "Don't concentrate all the power in one place. And, you know, this is partly, I think, what the framers also conceived. So it kind of is the line where political philosophy [begins]. You don't want all the power in the Government as opposed to the people. You don't want all the power in the Federal Government as opposed to the states."[25]

Rehnquist set up a law practice in Phoenix after finishing his clerkship. One story, perhaps apocryphal, has it that he could not decide whether to begin his practice in Phoenix or Albuquerque, so he flipped a coin and Phoenix won. Probably of more interest to analysis of his legal value scheme is the fact that on his way west from Washington to Phoenix he stopped in Fort Smith, Arkansas, to examine old court records and newspaper clippings on a man who appears to be one of Rehnquist's favorite historical figures, Isaac C. Parker, the notorious "hanging judge," who meted out 164 death sentences as a federal judge in the western district of Arkansas between 1875 and 1896. For fifteen of those years, until an act of Congress in 1891, no right of appeal was authorized. In a speech in 1983 before the University of Arkansas, Rehnquist recalled that, "I gathered some fascinating minutiae with a view to eventually writing a biography." In his interview with Jenkins for the *Times*, Rehnquist noted that "Judge Parker's trials were swift, and there was no appeal, but the fundamentals of due process were undoubtedly present."[26] Later in the interview Rehnquist had high praise for the English practice of allowing few appeals from trial-court judgments in criminal cases and of punishing those whose appeals are later deemed frivolous. Due process is important, he said, but society's moral judgments of its members must also be vindicated. Thus he chafes at the delays in executions caused by what he views as excessive appeals. In 1984 he boldly suggested that the automatic right of appeal be ended in federal civil cases.[27]

After starting his practice in Phoenix, Rehnquist continued his conservative activism, opposing (as will be discussed later) a local public accommodations law and, in 1967, an integration plan for the Phoenix public schools. He soon became friendly with another politically active, conservative Arizonan, Richard G. Kleindienst, and when President Nixon appointed Kleindienst deputy attorney general, Mr. Rehnquist was hired as head of the Office of Legal Counsel. In that role he screened the president's Supreme Court nominees—including Justices Burger and Blackmun. He also screened Clement F. Haynsworth and G. Harrold Carswell, who, as previously noted, were rejected amid major controversy and notoriety. Then, following the withdrawal of the names of Mildred L. Lillie and Herschel H. Friday (who presumably also had been screened by his office), Rehnquist himself was nominated in 1971.

In 1985, looking back on his thirteen-year tenure on the Court, Rehnquist insisted he had not changed his basic philosophical or ideological views since coming to the Court. On the other hand, he acknowledged that there has been some "growth" in his view of the Court's judicial decision-making process since he has been on the Court. "If you equate change with growth, then I think, in a sense there has been [some]," he said. "Maybe this is something that all members of collegiate courts go through." He went on, "When I first came here I had a feeling that these were kind of very critical jurisprudential battles in many of the cases. And, you know, I would get very kind of blue if I was in the minority a good deal, and feel very pleased if I was in the majority."

He next provided an important insight into the mind-set with which he entered the Court. "I think," he reflected, "I see it quite differently now from the perspective of 13 years. Then I used to think, you know, if there were an expression in a footnote in an opinion that I disagreed with, that we're going to be stuck with that footnote! But things have a way of evolving in a much more of a common-sense reaction to things than a strictly doctrinal approach, where A follows from B from C."

"I think I tend to view the process now as more of an

institutional one," he observed. "There probably are things to be said on both sides of issues that perhaps I didn't always think there were." There is, he thought too, a feeling present that "the institution has produced pretty well for 200 years, and it's undoubtedly going to survive very well without me or any of my colleagues in the future."[28]

It is difficult to escape the feeling of a sense of mission and the importance of self in promoting his ideological cause that was present at the time Rehnquist was named to the Court. Critics will, of course, see this as the mark of a zealot. Supporters, on the other hand, could interpret it as a complete dedication of the type necessary if the conservative or right-wing cause was to prevail in a nation then controlled by liberals and "secular humanists."

In any event, it is the goal of the remainder of this work to study the philosophical, legal, and ideological value system that constituted Chief Justice Rehnquist's intellectual baggage at the time he came to the Court. If, as the chief justice seems to insist, there have been no key changes in his intellectual firmament, such a study should prove valuable in analyzing his positions on cases that came before the Court while he was an associate justice and in anticipating his opinions and voting pattern in cases to come now that he has been named chief justice of the Court.

2

Political Theories and Labels

GIVEN the turbulence of the times and the general
public suspicion of President Nixon's motives at the
time of his nomination, Rehnquist received the kind
of detailed scrutiny of his legal and political philosophy that
few Supreme Court nominees are subjected to. Moreover, because of his job as the "president's lawyer's lawyer," he had
been in a position where he was required to present a wide
array of opinions on a multitude of subjects before official
bodies in the months preceding his nomination, which
helped to fuel the fires of controversy.

The Rehnquist presentations were done in a fashion that
made it difficult to ascertain whether the theories were his or
he was merely the conduit for the expression of the president's views. Of interest is the fact that during his confirmation hearings a clear pattern emerged in his political and legal views, and this pattern was commented on by a variety of
observers. After serving on the Court for a decade and a half,
both those views and Justice Rehnquist's basic philosophical
underpinnings remain basically unchanged. In short, his
opinions of today should come as no surprise to anyone who
paid attention to his earlier writings or public comments.

Labels have lost their meaning in our topsy-turvy world,
where, for example, Republican Ronald Reagan can spend
much of his campaign time clinging to the coattails of

Franklin D. Roosevelt, so it is clearly idle to speak, as people frequently do, of "liberals" and "conservatives" on the Supreme Court. As Herman Pritchett pointed out in his book *The Roosevelt Court,* the questions we must ask are, What does a conservative want to conserve? and What are the values that a justice or a nominee to the high court considers worth preserving or furthering? These are the critical questions.

When President Nixon announced the nomination of William Rehnquist as associate justice of the Supreme Court, he said that he had based the selection on two criteria: first, Rehnquist's excellence as a lawyer, and second, his "judicial philosophy." What the president meant by the first criterion is relatively clear, since Rehnquist was a successful, well-educated lawyer who was by general agreement intellectually equipped to compete on what Nixon called the "fastest track in the nation."[1]

It is when one gets to the second criterion, "judicial philosophy," that the president's meaning becomes much less clear. As he put it, "Now, I emphasized the word judicial . . . and by judicial philosophy, I do not mean agreeing with the President on every issue." He went on to say that a justice "should not twist or bend the Constitution in order to perpetuate his political and social view." Getting to the heart of the matter, the president emphasized that the nominee shared his judicial philosophy (he was a conservative), "but only in a judicial, not in a political sense." Mr. Nixon went on to give an example of what a conservative judicial philosophy meant to him. He explained: "As a judicial conservative, I believe that some Court decisions have gone too far in the past in weakening the peace forces as against the criminal forces in our society. The peace forces must not be denied the legal tools they need to protect the innocent from criminal elements."

In analyzing the president's statement, it can be seen that two critically important phrases often recur: "judicial philosophy" and "judicial conservative." While such terms may at first glance seem clear to a layman, Mr. Nixon's usage seems to violate traditional legal understanding of precisely

20

what these words connote. As Harvard's Alan Dershowitz pointed out when evaluating the president's law-and-order attitude, this is not a "judicial philosophy. It is just the sort of 'personal, political and social view' that the President emphasized should not be perpetuated by a Supreme Court justice."

A judicial philosophy, Dershowitz explained, deals with the role of the Court as an institution. "It is responsive to questions such as: What precedential weight should be given to prior decision? What power should the Court exercise over the other branches of the federal government and over the states? What tools of judicial construction should it employ in giving meaning to a constitutional or statutory provision?" In short, he points out, a judicial philosophy—"if it is truly judicial rather than 'political' or 'social'—does not speak in terms of giving the peace forces 'tools' to 'protect the innocent from criminal elements.' "

He goes on to emphasize that a "conservative" judicial philosophy is one that "respects precedent, and avoids deciding cases on constitutional grounds whenever a narrower ground for decision is available. Most important, a judge with a conservative judicial philosophy adjures employing the courts to effectuate his own political or social program—he is a decider of cases rather than an advocate of cases." A renowned judicial conservative, Oliver Wendell Holmes, described such a judge as one who has "no thought but that of solving a problem according to the rules by which he is bound" and who has learned "to transcend [his] own convictions and to leave room for much that he would hold dear to be done away with."

It is because of such problems, Dershowitz explains, that it is difficult to predict how a true judicial conservative will decide a given issue.

> For him, so much depends on how the issue is framed; on what the statute says; on the prior cases; on whether it arose in a Federal or state context. Justice Louis Brandeis was a judicial conservative, although a political liberal. Justice Holmes was a judicial and political conservative. But the judicial opinions of those giants tell us little

21

about their individual political views; for that we must go to their extra-judicial writings. Indeed, many people are surprised to learn how differently these men felt about the social and political issues of their day, since their judicial opinions were so similar.

In Dershowitz's view Justice James C. McReynolds, a bitter foe of New Deal legislation, represents the other side of the coin. He was a political conservative and a judicial activist. He went out of his way in his judicial decision making to strike down statutes that were, in his judgment, inconsistent with his economic and political views.[2]

Fred P. Graham, writing in the 3 November 1971 issue of the *New York Times,* approached the subject from a slightly different angle but ended by essentially agreeing with the analysis of the Rehnquist judicial philosophy suggested by Dershowitz. Graham began by reviewing the two thick binders of Rehnquist's writings lodged with the Senate Judiciary Committee during the confirmation hearings. These show, Graham explained, that while Rehnquist may be a political conservative, he clearly believes that a Supreme Court justice invariably writes his own view into the Constitution. In this Rehnquist differed markedly from the conservatives of the Court's recent past.

In the years just prior to the Rehnquist nomination, the leading lights of Supreme Court conservatism were Felix Frankfurter and John M. Harlan. Their typical complaint about the Court headed by Chief Justice Earl Warren was that it was too quick to write the liberal ideas of the justices into the Constitution, and they called for stricter adherence to *stare decisis.* As Graham pointed out, when President Nixon praised strict constructionist judges, he frequently cited Justice Frankfurter as the example to be followed.

Viewed in this light, said Graham, "Mr. Rehnquist, according to his own statements, is far from a strict conservative. Indeed, he is the type of judicial activist that Justice Warren was—except that Mr. Rehnquist believes that it is time to read conservative rather than liberal meanings into the Constitution."

22

To demonstrate this point, Graham quotes Rehnquist's own writings. "Nor is the law of the Constitution just 'there,' waiting to be applied in the same sense that an inferior court may match precedents," Rehnquist wrote in the *Harvard Law Record* of 8 October 1959. He went on, "There are those who bemoan the absence of *stare decisis* in constitutional law, but of its absence there can be no doubt. And it is no accident that the provisions of the Constitution which have been most productive of judicial lawmaking—the due process of the law clauses—are about the vaguest and most general of any in the instrument." Then, in a most telling summation of his judicial philosophy, Rehnquist explained, "It is high time that those critical of the present Court recognize with the late Charles Evans Hughes that for 175 years the Constitution has been what the judges say it is. If greater judicial self-restraint is desired, or a different interpretation of the phrase 'due process of law,' then men sympathetic to such desires must sit upon the high court."

Among other Rehnquist writings and speeches, Graham calls attention to a speech before the Newark Kiwanis Club. There, in discussing the young protesters' resort to civil disobedience to demonstrate their opposition to government policy, Assistant Attorney General Rehnquist told the group, "In the area of public law such disobedience cannot be tolerated, whether it be violent or nonviolent. . . . If force or the threat of force is required to enforce the law, we must not shirk from its employment."

Graham also showed that in speeches and congressional testimony Rehnquist had argued that the courts should play no role in shielding individuals from surveillance by government agents. Citizens, he said, would be protected by top officials in the executive branch or by Congress from errant or overzealous surveillance, and if aggrieved subjects of surveillance were allowed to go to court, this "would balance the scale too far against the interest of proper law enforcement." He also insisted that members of organized crime and subversives would abuse such court procedures to expose the government's surveillance efforts.

23

Precise terminology aside, from the beginning of the proceedings on Rehnquist's nomination, he was seen as a judicial activist, as an individual who scrupulously sought to enhance the powers and authority of the executive branch. It is important to recognize that there is a real distinction between a judicial activist and a judicial conservative, at least in the sense that Justice White and retired Justice Stewart are conservatives. Indeed, one of his former professors at the Stanford law school went even further in describing Rehnquist as "a bright, able, decent human being with a set of philosophical assumptions in favor of force and authority which only a few years ago we were calling 'Extremist.' "[3]

The question about Rehnquist that troubled and still troubles some observers is whether he is an extremist, not whether he is a liberal or a conservative. The latter two traditions have struggled with each other for dominance since the nation's beginnings. The liberal and conservative traditions, however, have typically been expressed by moderate men. Extremists, in the United States, have usually shouted their message from outside the political town-meeting, so to speak. So long as Americans thought of conservatives as tracing themselves from John Adams and liberals from Jefferson, the struggle for political control could be maintained without the excesses that threaten other nations by endangering reasonable political debate. On this point, John Adams once argued that "the mildness of government" in repressing its desire to punish those "ignorant, blundering thickskulls who are publishing radical manifestoes, is a pleasing, delightful characteristic, and though it will probably give encouragement to some disorders, it is too precious to be relinquished without absolute necessity."

But political control in the hands of an extremist could pose a serious threat to this tradition, and from the moment his nomination was announced there have been scholars and other observers who saw Rehnquist as a member of this different breed. Some, such as Tom Braden, thought from the first that Rehnquist's temperament had such a judicial cast.

24

On the basis of some of his testimony before various legislative committees while he was an assistant attorney general, electronic surveillance might be the least he would suggest for publishers of "radical manifestoes."[4]

One of the several paradoxes reflected in Rehnquist's political and legal theory was noted in 1971 by Professor Arthur S. Miller, then of George Washington University's National Law Center and a consultant to the Senate's Subcommittee on the Separation of Powers. At the time of the hearings on Rehnquist's nomination to the Supreme Court, Miller wrote: "That Rehnquist is very 'conservative' cannot be doubted. But he is hardly a 'strict constructionist.' His judicial cosmology has enabled him to give awesome expansions of presidential power while at the same time criticizing the Supreme Court decisions protective of the rights of suspected criminals."[5]

Others agreed that most certainly the future justice was no strict constructionist, if by that one meant someone who would agree with Mr. Justice Black's strict construction of the First Amendment's right of free speech.[6] In this they differed sharply from President Nixon's characterization of Rehnquist as a "strict constructionist," meaning a man who would merely "interpret" the Constitution. This probably also helps explain why the president, after earlier being openly critical of the Court, ended his nomination speech with a pious plea to the nation to respect the Court and its decisions (now that he had packed it). The problem with the president's characterization of Rehnquist is that it begs two key questions—first, what is he "strict" about? and second, what does "interpret" mean? Clearly, the most activist judge could validly argue that he is merely interpreting the Constitution, and Justice Black, the bête noir of the New Right and the conservatives, insisted to the end, and with considerable justification, that he was a "strict constructionist," especially with respect to the First Amendment.

At the time of his nomination, Rehnquist had taken what normally is a rather obscure office—assistant attorney general in the Office of Legal Counsel—and molded it into one of the most influential positions in the Nixon administration. He became the legal fireman who dutifully trudged to Capitol Hill to face questions by frequently hostile congressional committees and who sped about the country making speeches defending the Nixon administration's actions.

The noted constitutional historian Edward Corwin said in 1957 that the history of the American presidency has been one of gradual aggrandizement—at the expense of Congress, the judiciary, and the states. Under Nixon, Professor Miller noted, in less than three years the pace of that slow development significantly increased. It was Rehnquist who was the "resident theorist" who was able to find within the "crevices of constitutional law, ample justification" for whatever expansion of executive authority President Nixon desired. As Miller saw it, Rehnquist was able to be especially effective in this capacity because of his innate legal ability, coupled with a low-key manner and an unflappable approach that made him appealing both before Congress and on the lecture platform.[7]

The irony of this position—a Goldwater Republican supporting more governmental power over the individual and the economy—did not appear to disturb Rehnquist's serenity. In this respect, as Miller viewed him, he was an excellent model of the "legal apparatchik." The "apparatchik," as political scientists Zbigniew Brzezinski and Samuel Huntington have told us, is the government official who "must please superiors and prod subordinates, as contrasted with the politician, who must persuade equals." The question that troubled Arthur Miller and most other observers at the time of Rehnquist's nomination was whether his opinions as a lawyer stood for anything more than mere advocate's briefs, in which he simply presented a position without necessarily believing in it.

On this score the record seems to be mixed. Some of his presentations, such as his testimony in July 1970 before the Subcommittee on the Separation of Powers concerning the much-disputed concept of "executive privilege" drew grudging respect from such political opposites as Dean Acheson and W. Averell Harriman even though they strongly disagreed with his theory. On the other hand, in a later appearance before the same subcommittee, on 5 October 1970, Rehnquist's prepared statement defending a proposed allocation of new powers to the Subversive Activities Control Board was described in the press as "woefully inadequate."[8] His testimony did not even attempt to meet Senator Sam Ervin's objection that the new powers would be unconstitutional under the First Amendment. He did try, however, to show that the executive order creating the powers would not encroach on congressional power. The only member of the subcommittee who seemed convinced by the Rehnquist rationale was Republican Senator Edward Gurney.

While there was little or no question about Rehnquist's ability as far as legal technicalities were concerned, there were doubts about what might be called his potential judicial temperament. While coming from a variety of sources, questions about his ability to deal fairly with the larger problems facing society were the real issue. The point can best be made by noting Henry Steele Commager's observation that "great questions of constitutional law are great not because they are complicated legal or technical questions, but because they embody issues of high policy, of public good, or of morality."

In a highly heterogeneous society such as ours, the Supreme Court is constantly engaged in a cosmic juggling act, attempting to balance the many conflicting interests that make up the diverse society. To further complicate an already complicated situation, decisions in cases brought before the justices cannot be adduced by a simple reference to the Constitution or any logical extrapolation from a text written in 1789. As Oliver Wendell Holmes put it, justices of the Supreme Court must exercise "the sovereign prerogative of choices" between conflicting principles that typically are almost equally persuasive. How an individual fulfills the task of making these choices is the mark of a great jurist.[9]

Arthur Miller echoed the unease of many judicial scholars both then and now when he said at the time of Rehnquist's nomination:

> there is no *vade mecum* or table of logarithms by which he [a Supreme Court justice] can plot his course. He must, of necessity, weigh those conflicting interests and produce decisions that display, as that great judicial conservative Felix Frankfurter once said, both "logical unfolding" and "sociological wisdom." There can be little doubt about Rehnquist's ability as a logician; what is not known is the other half of Frankfurter's formulation.[10]

The question in most observers' minds at the time of the nomination hearings was, of course, whether Rehnquist had the capacity to grow with the postition, when his "client" became the people as a whole. There is some limited precedent for the notion that legally trained minds grow with the job. Legal lore has it that Lord Coke had been a tough, even mean-spirited, prosecutor for the Crown, but that upon being called to the bench he held that even the monarch himself was subject to the "critical reason of the law." For the United States, it is popular to cite as an example of this change in judicial outlook Oliver Wendell Holmes's periodic breaks with the president who had appointed him, Theodore Roosevelt. But a careful review of the history of the Supreme Court suggests that instances of this sort are the exception rather than the rule. As Arthur Miller gloomily but accurately observed at the time of the debates over Rehnquist's confirmation: "Despite the myth to the contrary, the Supreme Court (as with the presidency) has never been a place where men can or will grow 'larger.' People in public office tend to be essentially the same as they were before election or appointment. We don't like to believe this, but it is the lesson of history."[11]

During his confirmation hearings before the Senate Judiciary Committee, Rehnquist argued that he was being unfairly dubbed a reactionary. He insisted that he could divorce himself from any preconceptions and, as he put it, "let the chips fall where they may" in deciding cases on the bench. Moreover, he said that his visits to college campuses had taught him that "there was a very real fear" that the government was engaged in widespread spying on citizens, a fear that "could have a chilling effect on the freedom to communicate." But such fears, he said, were unfounded.

To support his qualifications to replace retired Justice John M. Harlan, he claimed to have argued successfully within the Justice Department for abandoning the novel claim that the federal government had the "inherent power," without court warrants, to wiretap domestic subversives. Rehnquist said he felt, however, that the government would fare better in a pending Supreme Court case—from which he said he would disqualify himself if confirmed—by arguing that antisubversion wiretaps could be made "reasonable," and thus constitutional, with self-imposed safeguards rather than through court supervision.

He also said that he had worked with other department lawyers to soften administration opposition to a "speedy trial" bill calling for dismissal of long-pending indictments in federal courts. Rehnquist said that he and others had demonstrated, however, that they were not "softies" by favoring legislation to cope with congestion in the criminal courts only if Congress would accept certain reforms sought by the administration.[12]

During the two days of hearings on his confirmation, Rehnquist engaged in a continuing tug-of-war with committee members such as Senators Edward Kennedy and Birch Bayh over whether his role as the lawyer for the attorney general and the president prevented him from spelling out most of his personal views of controversial administration policies. Senator Bayh in particular complained that he was being blocked in his efforts to explore the "judicial philosophy" that President Nixon had praised when he nominated Rehnquist. At one point Bayh said that if Rehnquist continued to insist that his lawyer-client relationship with administration officials precluded answers, he would write both the president and Attorney General Mitchell asking them to waive the client's privilege and let the government lawyer testify more fully.

Bayh's complaint prompted Senator Roman Hruska, a Nebraska Republican, to charge that committee Democrats were displaying a "newfound interest" in the philosophy of high-court candidates, contrasting sharply with their silence when liberal nominees were being confirmed, to which Bayh replied that "we have never had a president before who went on television and made judicial philosophy such a major consideration." Bayh and his allies, however, were largely unsuccessful in obtaining an insight into Rehnquist's judicial philosophy during or immediately following the hearings.

According to press accounts, Rehnquist, an experienced witness before congressional committees, remained calm as the senators spent nearly as much time in debating why he could not answer questions as they did in dealing with the questions themselves. At one point the nominee broke the tension by standing up and, with Chairman James Eastland's permission, walking once around the witness table to stretch his legs.[13]

The hearings were not without some embarrassing moments for the nominee, however. During the week of 11 November 1971, Senator Hruska, moving, as the *Washington Post* put it, "so swiftly that he seemed to supply an answer for which there had been no question," gratuitously introduced into the confirmation hearings a letter dated 9 November 1971 that on its face was supportive but that opened the door to a disclosure that eleven years before, Chief Judge Boldt of the federal district court in Tacoma, Washington, had charged the future Supreme Court nominee with "highly reprehensible" conduct. While it is not uncommon for a judge to lecture a lawyer practicing before him, Judge Boldt's criticism of Rehnquist was unusually vigorous. The trial record indicates that at one point the judge said: "I don't believe you were acting in good faith," and "I charge you with misconduct as an officer of the court." The judge went on: "I believe you deliberately have violated two different rulings of the court in a manner that is highly reprehensible, and I charge you with it and I believe it to be so. I am not going to punish you for contempt in this instance, but I regard it as contempt. Your attitude and the manner in which you have approached the matter, in my judgment, was a deliberate and flagrant violation of what you know to be the spirit of the ruling made."[14]

According to the *Washington Post,* Rehnquist, representing a former officer of an insolvent insurance company in a fraud trial, kept attempting to introduce evidence of a kind that Judge Boldt had already ruled was inadmissible. In conference in the judge's chambers, Rehnquist complained that Boldt had prejudged the case and asked for a mistrial. The judge replied: "Now, the ruling may be wrong, but a reputable attorney does not, after a ruling has been made, deliberately try to pettifog before the jury material that the court has ruled and said specifically and emphatically is not to be addressed to the jury, and that is what you did, and I believe you did it deliberately and with malice aforethought."

This Pandora's box was opened not by one of the nominee's critics but by a senator who was one of his staunchest supporters on the Senate Judiciary Committee and who commonly acted as the Nixon administration's spokeman on the panel. While some might see the maneuver as a practical demonstration of the old invocation, "God save us from our friends," the *Post* saw it as an attempt to cut his critics off at the pass and an indication of "the President's anxiety not to repeat the errors of two previous court confirmation campaigns."

Of crucial importance to an understanding of this episode is the fact that only one day after Mr. Nixon had announced the Rehnquist nomination he had nominated Boldt to be chief of the Nixon Pay Board. The letter, which the *Post* saw as "obviously solicited by the administration," began, "I do recall . . . " and went on to dismiss as a mere "misunderstanding" the judge's 1960 clash with Rehnquist "for what I considered disrespect to the court or something of that kind." In the 9 November letter to the Judiciary Committee, Boldt said that immediately after the incident in 1960 he repented and asked other lawyers to convey his apologies to Rehnquist.

Interestingly, Hruska did not provide the committee with the words from the court record in 1960, so the hearing was left uninformed about the seriousness of the encounter. One Rehnquist critic, Senator Bayh, told Hruska that he had heard something of the episode but had dismissed it as irrelevant and wondered why Hruska was so "uptight" about it. Hruska replied, according to the *Post*, that he had been "reliably informed that an issue would be raised and a disclosure would be made." He also said he knew that the press had been inquiring of Judge Boldt and the Justice Department concerning the details and noted that the judge's response was directed not to those inquiries but straight to the Judiciary Committee.[15]

Another instance involving questions about Rehnquist's pre-Court legal ethics came to light in the summer of 1986 at the time of the Senate Judiciary Committee's hearings on his nomination to be chief justice. At issue was the question of whether for two decades Justice Rehnquist had unethically concealed the existence of a trust fund that had been established to benefit his disabled brother-in-law. In this case it was the FBI that brought the matter to the attention of committee chairman Senator Strom Thurmond (R-S.C.), but the reason why it had taken the FBI years to uncover the matter was not explained. Moreover, of equal interest was the fact that the trust-fund issue was not raised during the committee's four days of confirmation hearings in late July 1986 or when its members approved the nomination on 14 August 1986.[16] The FBI did interview Rehnquist family members about the trust fund and reported its findings to committee members. On 25 August, Senator Thurmond said through a spokesman that he considered the matter closed. On 26 August 1986, however, four Democratic senators—Edward Kennedy of Massachusetts, Howard Metzenbaum of Ohio, Paul Simon of Illinois, and Alan Cranston of California—all of whom opposed the Rehnquist nomination, urged Thurmond to ask the FBI to reopen its inquiry and complete it within a week.

The situation seemed to be that while in private law practice in Phoenix, Arizona, Rehnquist had drawn up the trust agreement in 1961 at the request of his wife's dying father, Harold Davis Cornell, a San Diego physician. The trust set aside $25,000 for the benefit of Harold Dickerson "Dick" Cornell, Dr. Cornell's son and Mr. Rehnquist's brother-in-law. Dick Cornell, who was seventy-three in 1986, is a former San Diego prosecutor whose debilitating illness, multiple sclerosis, forced him to retire in 1962. As drafted by Mr. Rehnquist, the trust document provided that money was to be paid to Dick Cornell whenever his standard of living fell below the level he enjoyed when the trust was created. Cornell said that at that time he was earning about $50,000 a year from his law practice but that retirement had made a pauper of him—"It reached the point where I was making stew out of dog bones," he told the *New York Times*. He did not, however, learn about the existence of the trust fund for twenty-one years, according to the four senators.[17]

Cornell contended that Mr. Rehnquist knew of his plight but kept silent. Some legal scholars, as well as Cornell, assert that if the facts as presented are accurate, Mr. Rehnquist's inaction was particularly questionable, because he stood to gain if Cornell did not get the trust money. If Cornell died before obtaining the money, the trust fund was to be divided among his brothers and sisters, including Mr. Rehnquist's wife.[18]

While the Cornell matter is still unresolved at this writing, several points are worth summarizing in respect to Justice Rehnquist's past activities and views as they relate to the political label—conservative—frequently attached to the chief justice. His freewheeling approach to the judicial temperament is reflected in a variety of ways other than the Cornell controversy. Eleven years before his appointment to the Court, as a practicing attorney he had been charged by a federal district court judge with "highly reprehensible conduct." Moreover, during the 1971 hearings on his appointment to the Court he startled veteran legal scholars by insisting that his lawyer-client relationship with administration officials precluded him from spelling out his views on controversial administration policies.

Despite President Nixon's claim that he had appointed Rehnquist because of the justice's judicial philosophy, the record indicates that, in fact, the president selected him on the basis of Rehnquist's personal political and social views. These were the very factors that President Nixon had earlier insisted should not be factors in judicial appointments. It is difficult to predict how a true judicial conservative will decide a given issue, since, as Justice Holmes explained, a judicial conservative is one who has "learned to transcend [his] own convictions and to leave room for much that he would hold dear to be done away with."[19]

The emphatic consistency and predictability of Rehnquist's judicial voting behavior belies any meaningful application of the term "judicial conservative" to him. His record while on the Court and his published commentary elsewhere clearly indicate that he is a judicial activist of the type that Justice Warren was. The key difference between the two men is that Rehnquist wishes to read right-wing conservative meanings into the Constitution. Indeed, some legal scholars would go so far as to label Rehnquist an extremist, on the basis both of his activities while in the Justice Department and later as a member of the Court.

3

Media Views
on the
Rehnquist Philosophy

I N a 15 October 1971 editorial, the *New York Times* looked
carefully at the significance of Rehnquist's political, social, and economic philosophy. Such an analysis is important, the paper argued, since President Nixon "has by a
far greater degree than normal politicized the process of selection [of Supreme Court justices] and has so insistently pro-
claimed his determination to remake the Court in his own
image." That being the case, the paper said, "the Senate
needs to recall that its traditional deference to Presidential
nominations is an institutional courtesy rather than a constitutional command." The present nominees should not feel
unduly set upon, said the paper, since Mr. Rehnquist had
written earlier in the *Harvard Law Record* that the Senate
had an obligation to inquire into the basic philosophy of a
Supreme Court nominee.[1]

While in some abstract sense, the paper noted, "the Supreme Court should be above politics; yet it is obvious that
the Supreme Court deals with the stuff of politics." The paper
had repeatedly argued, it said, that while the president owed
it to the Court and the American People to keep partisan politics out of his judicial appointments, he also "ought to have
the broadest latitude in his selections *so long as they are*

made within the context of the American democratic system" (emphasis added). What this means, the editorial explained, "is that the candidate, whether liberal or conservative, of the right or of the left, must not be hostile to the broadly accepted principles of American constitutional democracy. This test, the Senate has the right and duty to make."

Of the two nominees being considered by the Senate, the choice of Lewis F. Powell, Jr., the paper concluded, presented relatively little difficulty, but "the same cannot be said for Mr. Rehnquist." The editorial conceded that Rehnquist was a capable lawyer of impressive academic and intellectual attainments. On the other hand, said the editorial, "his entire record casts serious doubt on his philosophic approach to that pillar of the American constitutional system, the Bill of Rights." Looking at every civil liberties issue—wiretapping, electronic surveillance, "no lock" entry, preventive detention, and the rights of the accused— "Mr. Rehnquist's record is appalling," the paper said. Moreover, he had scant respect for the individual's right to privacy under the Constitution; instead, he wanted to rely on "self-discipline on the part of the executive branch" to provide the protection needed. But, the paper asked, if self-discipline by the government were sufficient, why would the Founding Fathers have felt the need to provide the carefully defined safeguards of the Bill of Rights?

"What alarms us about Mr. Rehnquist," the editorial said, "is not the conservatism of his views . . . but our conviction on the basis of his record that he neither reveres nor understands the Bill of Rights." If this is so, "then he certainly does not meet the basic requirement that a justice of the Supreme Court be philosophically attuned to the irrevocable premise on which the American political structure rests: the protection of individual liberty under law, particularly against the repressive powers of government." Thus, while the Constitution leaves room for a wide diversity of political and social interpretations and judicial philosophies, there is a basic constitutional imperative that cannot be abridged or diminished by any governmental power, and that is respect for those basic issues of human freedom set forth in the first ten amendments. A belief in this fundamental principle is indispensable for service on the Supreme Court, the editorial insisted, and based on this premise, "Mr. Rehnquist's elevation to the Supreme Court could have a critically repressive effect on the constitutional protection of individual liberites for a long time to come. On Mr. Nixon's own premises, the Senate would be within its rights in insisting that while it may be content to accept a distinguished conservative like Mr. Powell, it is not obliged to accept a radical rightist like Mr. Rehnquist."[2]

The syndicated columnist William V. Shannon also addressed the problems growing out of the Rehnquist philosophy in an article in the 11 November 1971 issue of the *Times* entitled, "A Question or Three for Nominee Rehnquist." Shannon was particularly intrigued by the nominee's refusal to testify about his own views on the grounds that he had a lawyer-client relationship with President Nixon and Attorney General John Mitchell and that in testifying before congressional committees in the past he had been speaking not for himself but as an advocate for his client, the president. This was the same Rehnquist who, some years before in the *Harvard Law Record* had argued strenuously that it was the Senate's obligation at confirmation hearings to ascertain the philosophical underpinnings of a potential member of the Supreme Court.[3]

Mr. Rehnquist's rationale, said Shannon, struck most observers as remarkable in itself. Of course, the confidentiality of a lawyer's relation with a client is understood in private practice, where an attorney could reasonably represent either side in a case. "But," Shannon explained, "high Administration officials—such as Mr. Rehnquist—are generally expected to agree with programs they defend or else to resign." Reporters who covered Rehnquist's earlier testimony before congressional committees had little doubt that he agreed with the administration's position on law-and-order issues, said Shannon. Moreover, his law-journal articles and speeches, and the comments of his associates in private life, "indicate he held these views long before he joined the Administration."

While there was little doubt in Shannon's mind that both Rehnquist and Powell would receive Senate confirmation, he believed that body was confronted with problems associated with the Rehnquist nomination that it did not have to face in Powell's case. "The difference in response to the two nominations," Shannon explained, "arises from that elusive question of judicial philosophy. There is no doubt that if Mr. Rehnquist and Mr. Powell become justices of the Supreme Court, they will be found on the same side in many decisions. *What may differ is their approach to judging*" (emphasis added).

The difference, as Shannon saw it, was that "Mr. Rehnquist, 47, a member of Barry Goldwater's 'Arizona Mafia,' is, like his political patron, an ideological zealot given to writing letters to the editor and making public speeches in which he has vigorously defended a narrow set of strongly right-wing views. Rather than a judicial conservative reluctant to move away from established precedents or to deploy the powers of the Court aggressively, Mr. Rehnquist since his days as a law school student has had the record and reputation of a judicial activist eager to advance his political philosophy."

It seemed to Shannon that now that Rehnquist was faced with some hostility at his confirmation hearings, he was attempting to blur the sharp edge of his previously expressed opinions and theories. He was even careful to keep his voice at a monotone when he fenced with Senators Kennedy and Bayh. Moreover, he had clearly moderated his prior opposition to state and local public accommodations statutes and his prior support for "de facto segregation" in the public schools and various incursions into personal privacy. "My fundamental commitment, if I am confirmed," he told the Senate Judiciary Committee, "will be to totally disregard my own personal beliefs."

As Shannon saw it, to many liberal senators "this extreme formulation of a judge's need for intellectual detachment seemed implausible on its face." They were, however, faced with a real dilemma in the Rehnquist matter, for if they opposed a nominee of integrity and intellectual and professional competence because they disapproved of his personal philosophy and of the zeal with which he was likely to advance it, "will they be guilty of drawing the Supreme Court still further into the maelstrom of politics?"[4]

The plight that libertarian senators faced when dealing with the Rehnquist nomination also intrigued Tom Wicker, another syndicated columnist. In his column in the *New York Times* on 11 November 1971, Wicker said he considered the spectacle of Senator Edward Kennedy defending the reputation of William Rehnquist against allegations by Joseph Rauh of the Americans for Democratic Action to be suggestive of the painful dilemma in which liberals and civil libertarians had been placed by the Rehnquist nomination. This nomination, Wicker said, was not like that of Clement Haynsworth, whose record showed a lack of perception of possible conflict-of-interest situations. Nor was it like that of G. Harrold Carswell, in which the nomination hearings disclosed a glaring lack of qualifications for the Supreme Court. The Rehnquist matter was not even like that involving Lewis Powell.

"Mr. Rehnquist," said Wicker, "is a horse of a very different color," who at forty-seven could look forward to a long and active tenure on the Court. His record Wicker saw as that of a hardworking, vigorous champion of conservative political causes, but he was seen by persons on both sides of the political spectrum as being possessed with "superior intellect and skill in the law." It seemed likely that Mr. Rehnquist would become a driving force on the Court, and there were already those who saw him as becoming a more formidable leader than Chief Justice Burger in the conservative wing—a wing, Wicker pointed out, that may already have been in the majority on some issues and that almost surely would become dominant if Mr. Nixon should win another term.

This explained why liberals and libertarians were desperately casting about for ways to defeat Rehnquist. The hard fact, said Wicker, was that no evidence seemed to be forthcoming of the type that sank the Haynsworth and Carswell nominations or that led to the resignation of Abe Fortas. Thus, argued Wicker in his rebuke to Mr. Rauh, Senator Kennedy was hardly being sympathetic to a man of Rehnquist's views, but he was insisting that the nominee's basic integrity be unchallenged.

Then, getting to the nub of the problem over political and legal theory in the Rehnquist matter, Wicker explained that

> the real question before the Senate is whether it can, or should, reject Mr. Rehnquist solely because of his political views. On the one hand, the writers of the Constitution, in giving the Senate the power to confirm or reject presidential nominees to the judiciary, clearly meant the legislative branch to play a substantive role with the executive branch in this process, and to judge for itself the qualifications of a man to sit on the Supreme Court.
>
> On the other hand, to make that judgment solely on the basis of his political views (which, after all, may change) is dangerous business. It presumes some kind of rightful political orthodoxy; it would be to politicize the courts according to the temporary political coloration of Congress; it could punish some individuals for their ideas and frighten others out of having any.
>
> Moreover, it is bound to lead to retaliation, as it did when Republicans and conservative Democrats defeated President Johnson's nomination of Justice Fortas to be Chief Justice, at least partially on political grounds. Paying off that score had a good deal to do with Judge Haynsworth's subsequent rejection.

Wicker concluded by noting that some might argue that Mr. Nixon should not have handed the senators such a dilemma by appointing a political activist to a nonpolitical court, but the precedents are ample for such appointments. Moreover, the Senate would probably compound the damage if it denied Mr. Rehnquist his Court seat solely because of his political views.[5]

Another columnist who perceived the problems troubling American liberals in the nomination of William Rehnquist was Anthony Lewis, a longtime analyst of the American judiciary. In his 15 November 1971 column in the *New York Times,* Lewis saw some advantage in reviewing the words of Judge Learned Hand in his Holmes Lectures at Harvard. In the course of his remarks, Hand said: "Insofar as it is made part of the duties of judges to take sides in political controversies, their known or expected convictions or predilections will, and indeed should, be at least one determinant in their appointment."

As Lewis interpreted these remarks, Hand was not using the word "political" in its narrow, partisan sense but was saying that if our judges are to decide controversial national issues in the guise of lawsuits, then they will be chosen for their ideology. Furthermore, it is difficult for liberals to deny this premise, since for years they cheered the Supreme Court on as it advanced values of which they approved. Now a conservative president wanted a judge with different values. Is it logical or even democratic, Lewis asked, to deny him that power? After all, "the Presidential appointing power is the only means of seeing that the Court even distantly reflects the changing outlook of the country—as it must." To Lewis it was clear that a president should be allowed ample ideological scope in choosing a Supreme Court justice. Of course, there were limits—he thought, for example, that "a racist would be disqualified"—but the limits were broad. Thus he believed that many senators who entirely disagreed with Rehnquist's "right-wing ideas" would nevertheless "properly vote for his confirmation."

There is, however, a more basic issue remaining, and it is the one that most especially interested Judge Hand. This is, explained Lewis, the issue of the appropriate limits on the judicial function: "Should judges be dealing with heated social and economic controversies? Or should they limit themselves to tamer matters of more traditional law?" In recent years, Lewis said, questions of this nature have gone out of fashion, as had Justice Frankfurter's plea for judicial self-restraint, and this was most unfortunate, since "few seem to

41

remember the terrible lesson of the 1930's, when self-willed judges almost destroyed the Supreme Court."

We have replaced Frankfurter's philosophy of judicial self-restraint with what Lewis called the neo-realist view. This position was set forth with candor in 1958, the same year as Judge Hand's lectures at Harvard. It was enunciated, said Lewis, by Charles L. Black of Yale, who said: "We are told we must be very careful not to favor judicial vigor in supporting civil liberties, because if we do we'll be setting a bad precedent. Later on, we may get a bench of [conservative] judges . . . [but] suppose the present Court was to shrink from vigorous judicial action to protect civil liberties. Would that prevent a Court composed of latter-day McReynolds and Butlers from following their own views?"

Professor Black's rhetorical question assumed a negative response, but as Lewis viewed it, "it is not so clear that restraint on the part of a liberal Court would have no effect when the pendulum swings." He suggested as an example, Justice Brandeis, who was "the greatest intellect" who had ever sat on the Supreme Court and who had thought otherwise. "Again and again he held back from results that he personally desired because he thought he would encourage other judges to push their views in other cases," Lewis said.

Lewis admitted, however, that there is no convenient formula to use in setting limits on the judicial function, since every judge will have his own instincts about the values essential to the American system. Brandeis deferred to most legislative judgments, however foolish they appeared, but not when it came to privacy or freedom of speech, since Brandeis thought them too fundamental to the whole constitutional scheme, Lewis said.

Looking at the activist Warren Court, Lewis said he did not believe that the justices decided the great cases as they did out of "sheer perversity," as some of their sillier critics seemed to think. They were carrying out what they perceived to be their duty. Moreover, had they changed their minds because of anticipated harsh criticism, they might have been said to lack courage. Thus, as Lewis saw it, "The Warren Court is to be criticized not for its motives but, occasionally, for its judgment. It overreached from time to time," as in the *Miranda* case.

Then, giving us an insight into his criteria for judicial self-restraint, Lewis explained: "Judicial intervention on fundamental issues is most clearly justified when there is no other remedy for a situation that threatens the national fabric—when the path of political change is blocked. That was the case with racial segregation and legislative districting: it was not the case with Miranda."

Judge Hand, said Lewis, would have excluded all matters of that sort from the courts. Such a position, in Lewis's mind, is too drastic, since we have long come to rely on the Supreme Court as an essential medium of change in our rigid constitutional structure. "What we can ask of the judge is modesty, a quality required not only by man's imperfection, but by the fragile nature of the judicial institution," he concluded. Unfortunately for the reader, Lewis gave us no clue about whether he believed William Rehnquist had the qualities to which he referred.[6]

As the final days of the Rehnquist nomination hearings ground to a close, an interesting clash of views occurred between two nationally syndicated columnists over the intellectual capabilities and theoretical underpinnings of the newly named justice. The battleground was the *Washington Post,* and the contestants were Joseph Kraft, an internationally known political columnist, and the equally well-known political cartoonist, Herblock.

The exchange began with a column by Kraft in the 9 December 1971 issue. The controversy over the Rehnquist nomination reminded him, Kraft said, of a story about Justice Holmes, who, on being asked what he thought of the intellectual abilities of another judge, replied: "I never thought of him in that connection." That observation, Kraft said, suggested the nub of the "powerful, positive case" that could be made for Senate confirmation of Rehnquist. For years now, Kraft said, "hardly anybody has thought of the Supreme Court as performing an intellectual function." Then, in a remark that was to stir outrage and disagreement in many circles, Kraft went on, "Rehnquist, far more than any other recent nominee, has the caliber to restore intellectual distinction to the Court." To understand why, Kraft explained, it was necessary to say a word about the role of the Court in the United States. The country is dominated by the million-and-one daily actions of an energetic population largely unconstrained in its capacity to buy and sell, move and dream, educate and obscure, and build and tear down. Given the nearly universal disposition toward almost constant action, Kraft said, "It is ludicrous to think of tyranny being imposed on this country from above by some establishment eager to freeze the status quo or turn back the clock." (One wonders how Kraft would view this observation fourteen years later, with the forces of Ronald Reagan firmly in control.)

The central political problem of a populist country, as Kraft saw it, was "to preserve some modicum of elite values—respect for achievement; toleration for difference of outlook; regularity of procedure. Partly by original design, but even more by the chance accretions of history, the Court has come to be the defender of those values—the elitist institution in a populist country." But unfortunately for the Court, Kraft said, certain political decisions had been thrust upon it by the deadlock that had developed between the executive and legislative branches during the postwar period. In the fields of civil rights and legislative reapportionment, "the Court felt obliged—understandably, considering that all other avenues seemed closed—to make rulings that might much more appropriately have been the work of the President and the Congress."

"In the heady atmosphere engendered by those decisions," Kraft argued, "the Court headed by Chief Justice Warren became result-oriented." In case after case, it was "increasingly   hard   to   discover   the   inner   logic   of decision-making." According to Kraft, "Blacks seemed to be favored because they were blacks, baseball because it was a good, clean American sport, anti-trust plaintiffs because they were against economic monsters."

On the other hand, as Kraft saw it, Nixon's efforts to correct the imbalance had been "fumbling to the point of casting doubt on the sincerity of his claim to want 'strict constructionists.' " The president's preferred candidates had, before Rehnquist, been right-wingers, "so little distinguished that the Senate and the ABA have constrained him to throw them back in the pond." "Rehnquist," however, said Kraft, "is something else." He "has not shown sensitivity to the needs of people in trouble, and he has said some hardline—and to me silly-sounding—things about the influence of Supreme Court clerks and the softness of judges toward communism." "Some of these comments may be what ambitious juniors are required to say in order to get ahead in the Republican Party of Barry Goldwater and the Justice Department of John Mitchell." "Still," mused Kraft, somewhat grudgingly, "I suppose they represent a genuine right-wing conviction."

Another statement that was to incur the wrath of Herblock and others occurred when Kraft went on to say that "Rehnquist also has a mind of the highest candle-power. His comments in the Judiciary Committee hearing have been unfailingly lucid and discriminating. He has been 'hesitant'—a favorite word—when unsure of the fine details of a problem." Further, "even one of his staunchest opponents, Senator Kennedy, described him as 'a man with a quick, sharp intellect, who quotes Byron, Burke, and Tennyson, who never splits an infinitive, who uses the subjunctive at least once in every speech, who cringes when he sees an English word created from a Greek prefix and a Latin suffix.' " Then, to add fuel to the ire of his opponents, Kraft concluded:

> The Court does not now need more liberals, more conservatives, or more middle-of-the-roaders. There are enough of those to assure that nothing drastic is going to happen in civil rights or criminal law.
> What the Court needs is more brains. Rehnquist has

them—more abundantly perhaps than any present member. And by uplifting the quality of the Court in general, he will do far more than any particular decision in any particular case can do to advance the values thoughtful men hold dear.[7]

The Kraft article prompted an almost instantaneous response from Herblock, which took the form of a letter to the editor in the 10 December 1971 issue of the *Washington Post*. First, Herblock would have liked to see some specific cases to indicate that the Warren Court was lacking in the "inner logic of decision-making" that had permitted the court to favor blacks simply because they were blacks. Moreover, he called attention to the fact that Kraft had quickly brushed aside Rehnquist's earlier assertions about the sinister influence of left-wing clerks and the softness of judges on Communism.

It was Kraft's reference to Rehnquist's mind being of the "highest candle-power" and his being "hesitant . . . when unsure of the fine details of a problem," that prompted some ironic agreement from Herblock. Indeed, Rehnquist was hesitant in his testimony, said Herblock; he was " 'hestitant' to the point of admitting that he could not help the committee on the very kind of questions to which he had felt other nominees to the Court should respond."[8] Another thing that disturbed Herblock was Rehnquist's reply to the committee when he was asked about his record on minority rights in connection with public accommodations in Phoenix. He said, according to Herblock, "I think the ordinance really worked very well in Phoenix. It was readily accepted, and *I think I have come to realize since, more than I did at the time, the strong concern that minorities have for the recognition of these rights.* I would not feel the same way today about it as I did then" (emphasis added). That, in a nutshell, said Herblock, is the problem. "In those words Mr. Rehnquist displayed a candlepower that was dim but bright enough to illuminate the many things wrong with his record. He might change his views on the rights of a minority—not because they have those rights under the Constitution, but because

46

he sees now that they seem to feel strongly about those rights." This prompted Herblock to suggest a novel approach to judicial decision making: "the Court could perhaps have a good poll-taker ask of minorities: About rights, do you: (a) Feel strongly about them? (b) Moderately? (c) Not much? or (d) Don't know?"

Thus, Herblock said, "What anyone who understands the American system of justice might explain to Mr. Rehnquist and Mr. Kraft is that a judge is supposed to take into account the rights of everyone—including those who don't even know their rights, much less feel strongly about them. This is why Kraft in his little swipe at the 'Warren Court' didn't seem to understand that the Court was not protecting blacks as blacks, but rights as rights." Moreover, he went on, "It is hard to think of anything more important for a legal mind to grasp, unless he is, if I may paraphrase the words of Mr. Rehnquist's principal government 'client,' a loophole lawyer's loophole lawyer."

Kraft's comment that Rehnquist has brains, "more abundantly perhaps than any present member" of the Court, prompted a scoffing "Wow!!" from Herblock. As to Kraft's dismissing the need for more liberals, conservatives, or middle-of-the-roaders on the Court since "nothing drastic is going to happen in civil rights or criminal law," Herblock stoutly disagreed. If there is no likelihood of drastic changes on the Court, "President Nixon, the U.S. Senate and all of us interested citizens—including Joe Kraft—have been going to a lot of trouble for nothing," he concluded.[9]

In the same 10 December 1971 issue of the *Post* as the Herblock letter, Flora Lewis had a syndicated column that in one sense agreed with some of the points made by Kraft but, without mentioning either, ultimately seemed to support the basic constitutional position of Herblock. In discussing the Rehnquist appointment, she described it as an indication of a clear trend toward reinforcing the power of government and weakening the defenses of citizens against the abuse of authority. But "that is not conservatism," she insisted, relying also on a book by former justice Arthur Goldberg that had just been published. It is not conservatism, according to this point of view, because "there is little likelihood that a Nixon court will overrule what social and economic changes may be brought in for judgment," which is what the stoutly conservative Court did in President Roosevelt's early years.

As Lewis saw it, the Nixon Court, "as it is developing isn't likely to be one that challenges the decisions of Congress and the Executive. On the contrary, it is likely to be one which passively permits continued erosion of the individual's rights." Rehnquist, she felt, would be most supportive of this trend. "Rehnquist has made clear that he considers the government's 'need to govern,' that is, its right to defend its own authority, as superior to the citizen's rights protected by the Constitution. The First Amendment, he said in a speech on 19 March 1971, 'does not prohibit even foolish or unauthorized information-gathering by the government.' "

Given modern technology—which provides things like the electronic bug, computers, and a variety of required reports—the potential for government to invade the privacy of its citizens has increased enormously, Lewis pointed out. Yet "the sheer facts of modern life press on the individual and limit the freedoms he once took for granted. He needs more protection from the Constitution and the Court than he did in a pioneer or pastoral society, when government seldom touched him directly. But the way things are going, he is likely to get less. And this is not just until the next election or the one after that. A justice may serve for 25 or 30 years."

Lewis would concede that in the years just past, the Court had probably concerned itself with a variety of details of government that would better have been handled by the executive branch. But she concludes that the Rehnquist nomination suggests that the "danger now is that a restrained Court is going to restrain itself to the point of failing to fulfill its greatest function, the protection of the citizen against a too intrusive government."[10]

As might be expected, traditional conservative media

reaction to the Rehnquist nomination controversy differed markedly from the views just discussed. A brief sampling of the conservative approach will help give necessary balance to a complex constitutional controversy such as this.

The *National Review* observed in its 19 November 1971 issue that "the machine is turning on the new candidates for the Supreme Court, most conspicuously on Mr. William Rehnquist, and for most interesting reasons."[11] As the *Review* saw it, Mr. Rehnquist, judging from his writings, seemed to be saying not only that "the Warren Court strayed from the paths of constitutionalism, but that something ought to be done about it." While he had not said so in so many words, the *Review* thought he appeared to mean that there was no known reason why the Court should not re-orient itself. Moreover, the *Review* expected one of Rehnquist's critics to ask the inevitable question of whether he believed that he could turn back the clock.

The journal looked with favor on a Rehnquist position that it saw as opposing the "restoration of the Warren Court's liberal majority" because it would cause "not merely further expansion of the constitutional recognition of civil rights, but further expansion of the constitutional rights of criminal de-fendents, pornographers and demonstrators." These views of Rehnquist's were included in a letter he wrote to the *Washington Post* after the Senate's rejection of Carswell's nomination to the Supreme Court.

As the *National Review* saw it, this was "an exciting idea, which the liberals will need to cope with." On the one hand, liberals "believe in the freedom of a jurist to interpret the Constitution in either of the two dominant traditions, the so-called strict constructionist, and the social activist." "But," it went on, "it is implicit that they believe in social activism in behalf of fashionable objectives." "What about a jurist who is socially active in behalf of unfashionable objec-tives? We do believe they never thought of that," the editorial concluded.[12]

Two weeks later, the *National Review* published a verse entitled "Mr. Rehnquist's Coming Ordeal," by W. H. von

Dreele, which was in reality a thinly veiled attack on Rehnquist's critics. It read:

> Ravel's *La Valse*, you know it?
> At first, just fiddles bow it;
> Then dainty woodwinds try it,
> All straining to be quiet.
> Inexorably, others
> Join their orchestral brothers,
> Until the great finale
> Engulfs you with a volley.
> A similar crescendo,
> Replete with innuendo,
> Is building up to parry
> The man who went for Barry.[13]

In the same issue the *Review* saw both Rehnquist and Powell as coming through the Senate Judiciary Committee's hearings with "their ethical and intellectual qualifications unimpaired." But, it warned its readers, "the real—that is, the ideological—fight was just beginning, particularly as regards Rehnquist."[14] This did not trouble the publication, since it considered it "a relief to get down to the real issue, marked as it has been in the recent past by charges of mediocrity and, in the case of Clement Haynsworth, by trumped-up allegations of 'conflict of interest.' " Now, said the journal, "We will discover whether Richard Nixon is going to be permitted to alter the direction of the Court, as he promised to do during the 1968 campaign, an intention he has since reaffirmed."

No one, as the *Review* saw it, needed to worry that any Court would overrule *Brown* v. *Board of Education* or any of the other major civil rights cases, since all the present and the prospective justices seemed to be in "striking" unity on these decisions. On the other hand, as the journal viewed the prospective Court it did not see it as one "likely to press forward with new initiatives in the area of race relations."

Why, then, the concern and opposition resulting from the Rehnquist appointment? the *Review* asked rhetorically. "At its serious philosophical level," said the editorial, "the fight is really over the relative weight of the Bill of Rights—or, rather, the Bill of Rights as read through the prism of the Fourteenth Amendment—within the constitutional framework as a whole." Our constitutional tradition from its very beginning has contained "a tension between individual rights and liberties on the one hand and the goals expressed in the Preamble [to the Constitution] on the other," the journal explained. It went on:

> The First Amendment, read through the prism of the Fourteenth, can be taken as establishing a "right" of "free speech" even though the Bill of Rights contains no reference to free speech. The "equal protection" clause of the Fourteenth can be read as implying a "right" to equal medical care, equal education, equal housing or even equal income. The "due process" clause of the Fourteenth can be interpreted in ways that make criminal prosecution excruciatingly difficult.[15]

As the *National Review* saw it, "This particular reading of the Constitution has allowed the courts to bypass Congress in the pursuit of various social and political goals."

The major problem with the position just outlined, said the editorial, was "What happens to the goals of the Preamble, such as 'to insure domestic tranquility,' or 'to establish justice,' or 'to provide for the common defense'?" In its judgment, it was these goals for which our constitutional system was designed in 1787. Moreover, it said, not only was there no Bill of Rights in the original Constitution, but "all the delegates voted unanimously *not* to adopt one."[16]

It is in the context of this clash of constitutional doctrines that the dispute over the Rehnquist nomination must be seen, said the *Review*. "Rehnquist, to put it one way, is a Preamble man. He would shift the emphasis some distance toward 'insuring domestic tranquility,' 'securing justice,' and the like. Using President Nixon's language, the paper said, "Rehnquist's nomination is meant to strengthen the 'peace forces' as against the 'criminal forces' in the nation. The framers of the Constitution would have recognized this as a perfectly legitimate objective."

As the journal saw it, the fight over the nomination was likely to get rough, because profound issues and interests were at stake. This was especially true because the Court was at the "tipping-point" on a number of issues concerning due process and equal protection. In the editor's opinion, "Rehnquist himself embodies the counterinterpretation most clearly. And the confirmation of *both* Rehnquist and Powell would tip the Court in the direction Nixon and, doubtless, the nation desires."[17]

Robert L. Bartley, writing in the *Wall Street Journal,* produced another approach highly supportive of the Rehnquist nomination. As he looked at the controversy, he concluded that "the most powerful impression to emerge from the microscopic public analysis of the life and works of Supreme Court nominee William H. Rehnquist is that his critics are pretty desperate. At one point the arguments and innuendos offered by critical witnesses proved too much even for the most critical Senators, and Sen. Edward Kennedy upbraided the witnesses for creating 'an atmosphere which I think is rather poisonous.' "

Bartley focused particularly on the charge by some of his critics that Rehnquist was "outside the mainstream of American thought and should not be confirmed." This, said Bartley, is "a fascinating proposition. How can someone with legal standing and personal integrity fit to grace the Supreme Court be that far out of the mainstream? What would be the opinions of a man who is such a pillar of the bar and still fails to understand the Bill of Rights?" He then proceeded to note briefly and summarily dismiss most of the criticism that had emerged during the hearings.

In addressing the charge that Mr. Rehnquist's views were extreme, Bartley observed that "if Mr. Rehnquist's opinions [on no-knock raids and preventive detention] here are outrageously extreme, it would seem, so are the opinions of the majority of the Senate Judiciary Committee. Similarly, if his defense of the constitutionality of such laws as 'no-knock' raids and 'preventive detention' in the District·of Columbia are out of the mainstream, the mainstream does not include the majority of both houses of Congress."

Finally, Bartley ridiculed criticism of the nominee's record on racial matters. "Mr. Rehnquist's extremist position on civil rights, then, turns out to be nothing more than the familiar proposition that the Constitution is color-blind." Thus, he concludes, "as the Senate debates the nomination, it seems, it will have to decide more than whether it's proper to weigh a nominee's philosophy. It also needs to weigh whether words like 'extreme' and 'out of the mainstream' better describe Mr. Rehnquist's philosophy, or the position his critics have been forced to take to oppose him."[18]

In summary, it can be said that several major national newspapers sharply opposed the Rehnquist appointment while at the same time supporting the appointment of Justice Powell, whom they acknowledged to be a conservative of a different sort. Conceding that Rehnquist was a capable lawyer, the *New York Times,* for example, saw the Rehnquist record on the guarantees contained in the Bill of Rights as "appalling." What alarmed the *Times* was not the conservatism of his views but the paper's conviction that Rehnquist "neither reveres nor understands the Bill of Rights." Thus he did not meet the basic requirement for the position—"that a justice . . . be philosophically attuned to the irrevocable premise on which the American political structure rests."[19]

Many of the nation's leading syndicated political columnists, while not enthusiastic about the appointment, at the same time perceived major constitutional difficulties confronting senators who might oppose the nomination primarily on ideological grounds. Some, such as William V. Shannon, however, were intrigued by Rehnquist's refusal to testify about his own views because of what he called a "lawyer-client" relationship with President Nixon, while earlier he had argued in the *Harvard Law Record* that it was the Senate's obligation to ascertain the philosophical underpinnings of a potential member of the Supreme Court. What worried other observers was that because of Rehnquist's capabilities as a lawyer, his sharp mind and driving personality made it likely that he would become a leading force on the Court and that his particular brand of conservatism would dominate it.

Traditionally conservative news media unsurprisingly supported the Rehnquist nomination enthusiastically. They believed that Rehnquist would help lead the way toward the Court's reorienting its position and would stop the "further expansion of the constitutional rights of criminal defendants, pornographers and demonstrators," as the *National Review* put it. Moreover, that journal questioned the legitimacy of the "Incorporation Doctrine" of the Fourteenth Amendment, which dated back to the 1920s and in which provisions of the Bill of Rights were applied to the states. That publication thought that Rehnquist might fight to halt this trend, since in its judgment he would emphasize provisions of the Constitution's Preamble stressing "domestic tranquility" and "securing justice" because, as that journal put it, "Rehnquist . . . is a Preamble man."[20]

Writing in the *Wall Street Journal,* Robert Bartley warmly supported the Rehnquist nomination, finding that his critics had become desperate because of their inability to find anything substantial enough to be used to deny him confirmation. Bartley indicated profound disbelief that someone with legal standing and personal integrity could be outside the mainstream of American political thought. Moreover, Bartley believed that the criticism of Mr. Rehnquist's alleged extremist position on civil rights resulted merely from what Bartley perceived to be Rehnquist's view that the Constitution was color-blind.

In short, the media debate over the Rehnquist appointment centered not on his intellect and legal credentials but on his alleged lack of judicial temperament and his ideological rigidity.

54

4

Mr. Justice Rehnquist
and Civil Liberties

DURING the last week of December 1984, as one viewed the American Broadcasting Company's documentry "Closeup," which broadcast Justice Rehnquist's first television interview since being appointed to the Supreme Court by President Nixon twelve years before, one was struck by the casual acknowledgment that the current Court probably had "decided some cases against claims of civil liberties that perhaps the Warren Court might have decided the other way." But, the justice added, "I don't regard that as an unfortunate chipping away of civil liberties because typically, the way that sort of charge is phrased suggests that the maximum number of civil liberties claims ought to be granted, which would just be a recipe for anarchy that isn't called for by the Constitution at all."

Even though Justice Rehnquist has actively sought to institute a variety of new social and judicial policies since being on the Court, most of his off-Court writings decry the notion of a living Constitution resulting from an activist Court. In a 1976 *Texas Law Review* article he attacked what he perceived to be the activist's rationale based on the proposition that "judges, as a whole, have a role of their own, quite independent of popular will, to play in solving society's problems."[1] The expression of this view is usually accompanied by a "sophisticated wink," he says, since we are all familiar with Chief Justice Charles Evans Hughes's famous aphorism, "We are under a Constitution, but the Constitution is what the judges say it is."[2]

Rehnquist described the activists as saying essentially that "any sophisticated student of the subject knows that judges need not limit themselves to the intent of the framers, which is very difficult to determine in any event. Because of the general language used in the Constitution, judges should not hesitate to use their authority to make the Constitution relevant and useful in solving the problems of modern society."[3] But, he wrote, there are "at least three serious difficulties [that] flaw [this] version of the living Constitution. First, it misconceives the nature of the Constitution, which was designed to enable the popularly elected branches of government, not the judicial branch, to keep the country abreast of the times. Second, [this] version ignores the Supreme Court's disastrous experiences when in the past it embraced contemporary, fashionable notions of what a living Constitution should contain. Third, however socially desirable the goals sought to be advanced by [this] version, advancing them through a freewheeling, non-elected judiciary is quite unacceptable in a democratic society."[4]

In Justice Rehnquist's view, the Constitution that the Founding Fathers drafted was intended to endure indefinitely, so in that sense it is a living document. But the Founders' view differed from today's activist's view in that the Founders' "very well-founded hope was the general language by which national authority was granted to *Congress and the Presidency. . . .* These two branches were to furnish the motive power within the federal system, which was in turn to coexist with the state governments; the elements of government having a popular constituency were looked to for the solution of the numerous and varied problems that the future would bring" (emphasis added). There were, indeed, limits placed on all governments, in part to protect individual rights. But, he insisted, "these limitations . . . were not themselves designed to solve the problems of the future, but were instead designed to make certain that the constituent branches, when *they* attempted to solve those problems, should not transgress these fundamental limitations."[5]

As the New Right's favorite on the Supreme Court, and sometimes erroneously labeled a conservative, Justice Rehnquist has been a leader in the high court's rejection of civil liberties claims in recent years. In the television interview he described such claims as "essentially anti-majoritarian," just as the Constitution is "in a sense, anti-majoritarian." He went on to observe, "that certainly doesn't mean that every time a case comes to this court where the term 'civil liberties' is invoked, the court ought to unthinkingly decide in favor of the civil liberties claimant." On the same program, New York University law professor John Sexton remarked that the trend Justice Rehnquist was alluding to was "an alarming thing because it's the court's job to protect minorities and to protect individual liberties against institutions and especially against government."[6] At issue were recent decisions where the majority of justices took a key step toward allowing preventive detention before trial, enabled prosecutors to use illegally seized evidence, gave prison guards the unrestricted power to search inmates, granted several forms of government aid to religion, allowed colleges receiving federal money to discriminate against women in nonsubsidized programs, and approved greater leeway for police officers to search vehicles, homes, and open fields. In all these cases, Justice Rehnquist either took a leading part or supported the majority.

In his study, *Democracy in America*, Alexis de Tocqueville argued that lawyers would secure the new state against the excesses of democracy. "They derive from their occupation certain habits of order," he wrote. These include "a taste for formalities, and a kind of instinctive regard for the regular connection of ideas which naturally render them very hostile to the revolutionary spirit and the unreflecting passions of the multitude."[7] If de Tocqueville had known Rehnquist, he might not have felt it necessary to devote a whole chapter to this argument. He could have pointed to Rehnquist as a native example of his contention that "lawyers value legality more than freedom, are not altogether averse to tyranny," and, "provided the legislature undertakes of itself to deprive men of their independence, are not dissatisfied."[8]

Interestingly enough, these facets of the justice's theoretical pattern were thoroughly aired at the time his nomination was being considered by the Senate and were not smuggled onto the Court surreptitiously. For example, on 5 May 1971 Rehnquist, in discussing his novel doctrine of "limited martial law" before a North Carolina audience, defended as constitutional and proper the arrest of demonstrators during the May Day disturbances in Washington, D.C., even though the police had not fulfilled the ordinary requirement of bringing the suspects before a magistrate for arraignment within a reasonable time. As Assistant Attorney General Rehnquist then explained it, had the police done that, there would not have been any patrolmen left to arrest other violators. Critics of the arrests said that they were basically police sweeps of both the innocent and the guilty in order to break up the demonstration and discourage others from taking part. In fact, after the dust and the emotions of the moment had settled, the vast majority of the several thousand people arrested either were never charged or were found innocent.[9]

This was not the first instance in which Rehnquist formally expressed himself on the subject of demonstrators. In a Law Day address in Newark, Delaware, in 1969 he referred to some of them as the "new barbarians." As he saw it then:

> The very notion of law, and of government of law, is presently under attack from a group of new barbarians. They are found today on university campuses, in various public demonstrations and protests and elsewhere, though they represent only a small minority of the numbers participating in these movements. Just as the barbarians who invaded the Roman Empire neither knew nor cared about Roman government and Roman law, these new barbarians care nothing for our system of government and law. They believe that the relatively civilized society in which they live is so totally rotten that no remedy short of the destruction of that society will suf-

fice. . . . I suggest to you that this attack of the new barbarians constitutes a threat to the notion of a government of law which is every bit as serious as the "crime
wave" in our cities.[10]

Later, in testimony before the Senate Constitutional
Rights Subcommittee on 9 and 16 March 1970, Rehnquist
argued that the government had a right to collect data about
individuals, that such a practice was constitutional, and that
the remedy against a general abuse of the practice was restraint on the part of the executive branch. In defending the
government's right to spy on its citizens, Rehnquist conceded that it would probably be a waste of taxpayers' money
to use electronic surveillance to spy on the committee chairman, Senator Sam Ervin, in apparent recognition of the senator's conduct in peace and war. While such a practice might
be wasteful, there was nothing illegal or unconstitutional
about it, as Rehnquist saw it. In a later public address, however, he set forth a more moderate and reasonable statement
of the government's right and duty to gather information.[11]

Shortly afterward, on 1 July 1970, Assistant Attorney
General Rehnquist told the House Foreign Affairs Committee
that the president has the constitutional power to commit
American troops to battle without seeking congressional as-
sent. He acknowledged that unanimity with Congress on
such a commitment was desirable but went on to note that
"this is not to say, however, that Congress must always be
consulted before American armed forces are deployed or
committed to hostilities abroad. There are numerous instances in our history in which Presidents have deployed
armed forces outside of the United States in a way which
invited retaliation from a foreign power."[12]

Speaking on the same subject on 28 May 1970 before the
New York City Bar Association, Rehnquist first posed and
then answered three leading questions central to the dispute:

> First, may the United States lawfully engage in
> armed hostilities with a foreign power in the absence of a
> congressional declaration of war? I believe that the only

supportable answer to this question is "Yes." Second, is the constitutional designation of the President as Commander in Chief of the armed forces a grant of substantive authority, which gives him something more than just a seat of honor in the reviewing stand? Again, I believe that this question must be answered in the affirmative. Third, what are the limits of the President's power as Commander in Chief, unsupported by congressional authorization or ratification of his acts? It is scarcely a novel observation to state that the limits of the power are shadowy indeed. But I submit to you that one need not approach anything like the outer limits of his power, as defined by judicial decision and historical practice, in order to conclude that it supports the action that he took in Cambodia. . . . It has been recognized from the earliest days of the republic by the President, by Congress and by the Supreme Court that the United States may lawfully engage in armed hostilities with a foreign power without a congressional declaration of war. Our history is replete with instances of "undeclared wars," from the war with France in 1798 through 1800, to the Vietnamese war. . . . These activities represent three separate facets of the historical exercise of the power as Commander in Chief by various Presidents—the power to deploy armed forces outside of the United States; the power to engage United States armed forces in conflict with a foreign nation; and the power to determine how a war, once initiated, shall be conducted.[13]

These statements were in keeping with the views expressed by Mr. Rehnquist in 1970 in the *New York University Law Review,* where he argued in support of President Nixon's unilateral action in sending American troops into battle in Cambodia. There he said:

The President's determination to authorize incursion into these Cambodian border areas is precisely the sort of tactical decision traditionally confided to the Commander in Chief in the conduct of armed conflict. From the time of the drafting of the Constitution it has been clear that the Commander in Chief has authority to take prompt action to protect American lives in situations in-

volving hostilities. . . . A decision to cross the Cambodian border, with at least the tacit consent of the Cambodian Government, in order to destroy sanctuaries being
utilized by North Vietnamese in violation of Cambodia's
neutrality, is wholly consistent with that obligation.[14]

In the related area of the executive's appointive authority, it was Rehnquist who drafted President Nixon's letter to
Senator William Saxbe of Ohio at the time of the Carswell
nomination debate arguing that the president has the right to
put whomever he pleases on the Supreme Court, regardless
of the Constitution's express proviso for the advice and consent of the Senate in this process. The letter's rationale supporting the president's appointment power presented such
convoluted thinking that it prompted one observer to conclude that it must have caused high school civics students to
wonder whether their president could read plain English.[15]

Over a decade later, and as a sitting Supreme Court justice, he addressed himself again to this subject at a critical
point in the 1984 presidential election race when Republicans were generally attempting to defuse the public concern
that a Reagan victory in the campaign would result in his
packing the federal courts, especially the Supreme Court,
with extreme conservatives. Speaking at the University of
Minnesota College of Law on 19 October 1984, he said that

> a President who sets out to "pack" the Court seeks to
> appoint people to the Court who are sympathetic to his
> political or philosophical principles. There is no reason in
> the world why a president should not do this. One of the
> many marks of genius which our Constitution bears is
> the fine balance struck in the establishment of the judi-
> cial branch, avoiding both subservience to the sup-
> posedly more vigorous legislative and executive
> branches, on the one hand, and to total institutional iso-
> lation from public opinion, on the other. The perform-
> ance of the judicial branch of the United States govern-
> ment for a period of nearly two hundred years has shown
> it to be remarkably independent of the other coordinate
> branches of that government. Yet the institution has
> been constructed in such a way that the public will, in

61

the person of the President of the United States—the one official who is elected by the entire nation—have something to say about the membership of the Court, and thereby indirectly about its decisions.[16]

After reviewing a history of presidential attempts to "pack" the Court to insure the institutionalization of their political, economic, or social theories, Justice Rehnquist concluded that this had been something of an ineffective exercise of executive power. As he explained it:

Thus history teaches us, I think, that even a "strong" President determined to leave his mark on the Court—a President such as Lincoln or Franklin Roosevelt—is apt to be only partially successful. Neither the President nor his appointees can foresee what issues will come before the Court during the tenure of the appointees, and it may be that none had thought very much about these issues. Even though they agree as to the proper resolution of current cases, they may well disagree as to future cases involving other questions when, as judges, they study briefs and hear arguments. Longevity of the appointees, or untimely deaths, such as those of Justice Murphy and Justice Rutledge, may also frustrate a President's expectations; so also may the personal antagonisms developed between strong-willed appointees of the same President. All of these factors are subsumed to a greater or lesser extent by observing that the Supreme Court is an institution far more dominated by centrifugal forces pushing towards individuality and independence than it is by centripetal forces pulling for hierarchial ordering and institutional unity. The well-known checks and balances provided by the Framers . . . have supplied the necessary centrifugal force to make the Supreme Court independent of Congress and the President. The degree to which a new Justice should change his way of looking at things when he "puts on the robe" is emphasized by the fact that Supreme Court appointments almost invariably come "one at a time," and each new appointee goes alone to take his place with eight colleagues who are already there. . . . A second series of centrifugal forces is at work

> within the Court itself, pushing each Member of the
> Court to be thoroughly independent of his col-
> leagues. . . . When one puts on the robe, one enters a
> world of public scrutiny and professional criticism which
> sets great store by individual performance, and much
> less store upon the virtue of being a "team player."[17]

Of course, some observers may see an address like this,
given as it was in the midst of a presidential campaign and on
a subject central to the campaign, as an opening move in
Justice Rehnquist's bid to become chief justice when that
position became open.

In his role as assistant attorney general, Rehnquist had a
chance to present his views on the role of the president as the
chief administrator of the nation. On 18 September 1970 he
is quoted as saying, after incidents in which federal employee
groups criticized President Nixon's policies: "The government as an employer has a legitimate and constitutionally
recognized interest in limiting public criticism on the part of
its employees even though that same government as a sovereign has no similar constitutionally valid claim to limit dissent on the part of its citizens."[18]

In an even more controversial vein, in discussing problems of unreasonable searches he later said:

> In view of the very nature of the investigative proc-
> ess, it would be highly unrealistic to require that there be
> "probable cause" to suspect an individual of having
> committed a crime in order that his activities may be
> inquired into in connection with the investigation of the
> crime. Quite the contrary, probable cause—for an arrest
> or specific search—is hopefully to be found at the *conclu-
> sion* of an investigation and ought not to be required as a
> justification for its *commencement.* The basic limitation
> which may properly be placed on investigative authority
> is that it must be directed either to the solution or to the
> prevention of a crime, and that it pursue leads reasona-
> bly believed to aid in that activity.[19]

One of the central propositions guiding Rehnquist's legal philosophy both before and after his appointment to the Supreme Court is the view described by David Shapiro that conflicts between the individual and the government should, whenever possible, be resolved against the individual and in favor of government authority. In supporting the concept of pretrial detention, Rehnquist said on 4 December 1970 that to protect society from "persons who pose a serious threat to life and safety" while they are awaiting trial, "I think that the pretrial detention concept represents a rational and constitutional solution to a complex problem."[20] He explained his view as follows:

> I believe that society has the right to protect its citizens, for limited periods through due-process procedures, from persons who pose a serious threat to life and safety. We do not prevent wanton misconduct by dangerous recidivists during pretrial release. I believe the pretrial-detention provision of the D.C. crime bill accomplishes this result in a manner entirely consistent with the spirit and the letter of the U.S. Constitution.[21]

In the same vein, on 15 July 1971 Rehnquist defended government wiretapping under court order in criminal cases and without court order in national security cases. As he posed the issue, "Is the invasion of privacy entailed by wiretapping too high a price to pay for a successful method of attacking this and similar types of crime? I think not, given the safeguards which attend its use in the United States."[22]

In a related area of criminal procedure, Rehnquist testified before the Senate's Constitutional Rights Subcommittee that he favored "an effort by statute to modify all or part of the exclusionary rule which now prevents the use against a criminal defendant of evidence which is found to have [been] obtained in violation of his constitutional rights." In the same testimony he said that the plethora of opportunities for a defendant to stall through repeated use of habeas corpus proceedings should be limited.

Rehnquist's support of government authority over individual rights was reflected in a variety of speeches during his days in the Justice Department. On 29 June 1971 he defended the executive privilege to deny information of certain kinds to Congress. Shortly afterward, on 5 October 1971, he supported the legality of reviving the Subversive Activities Control Board by transferring to it Justice Department powers to designate organizations as Communist. At the same time he argued in favor of mail curbs on allegedly pornographic material.[23]

One of his more revealing public utterances during this period is found in his letter of 14 February 1970 to the *Washington Post* attacking the newpaper's editorial opposing the Supreme Court nomination of G. Harrold Carswell. The newspaper, Rehnquist charged, was fighting for "the restoration of the Warren Court's liberal majority. . . . In fairness you ought to state all of the consequences that your position logically brings in train: not merely further expansion of the constitutional recognition of civil rights, but further expansion of the constitutional rights of criminal defendants, of pornographers and demonstrators."[24]

That Rehnquist tended to be intemperate in his political and legal rhetoric prior to putting on the robes of a Supreme Court justice is difficult to deny. For example, this was one of several complaints against him raised by Joseph Rauh, speaking for the Leadership Conference on Civil Rights before the Senate Judiciary Committee's hearings on his nomination. Rauh, who was not immune to ideological hyperbole himself, called Rehnquist a "laundered McCarthyite" who had charged the Warren Court with sympathy toward Communists. He said Rehnquist had raised a false issue of attorney-client privilege in declining to give his own version of statements he had made as a Justice Department spokesman and administration witness in Congress, though he freely waived the privilege when he wanted to tell of his influence in softening the administration's position on wiretapping. Rauh also charged that Rehnquist was willing to violate the Supreme Court's own confidentiality in a 1957 article about the secret "inner workings" of the Court.

Rauh—who was, like Rehnquist, a former high-court law

clerk—said that Rehnquist compared unfavorably with retired Justice John M. Harlan, whom he would replace if confirmed. He noted that Harlan had written an opinion for the
Court the previous term on a search-and-seizure issue, and
Rehnquist had testified that the ruling was on a "technical-
ity." He said Harlan, a conservative, had written some of the
important civil liberties opinions that Rehnquist had criticized in an article that began:

> Communists, former Communists and others of like
> political philosophy scored significant victories during
> the October, 1956, term of the Supreme Court
> . . . culminating in the historic decisions of June, 1957.
> In two opinions handed down in early May, 1957, the
> Court held that two applicants to take bar examina-
> tions—one an admitted ex-Communist and one identi-
> fied as a Communist—had been deprived of constitu-
> tional rights by the respective state bars when the latter
> refused to let them take the examination. . . .
> A decision of any court based on a combination of
> charity and ideological sympathy at the expense of gen-
> eral rules of law is regrettable no matter whence it
> comes. But what could be tolerated as a warm-hearted
> aberration in the local trial judge becomes nothing less
> than a constitutional transgression when enunciated by
> the court of the land.[25]

On the same day that these sharp attacks on Rehnquist's
political and legal theories were being launched by the
Leadership Conference on Civil Rights, Rehnquist himself
was moving to squelch other criticisms directed toward his
alleged right-wing tendencies. Responding to reports that he
had belonged to the John Birch Society while living in
Phoenix, Rehnquist filed an affidavit with the Senate Judiciary Committee swearing that he was not now and had not
been "at any time in the past" a member of that rightist
organization.[26]

When Rauh, in his testimony later that day, suggested
that Rehnquist had failed to disavow completely any "con-
nections" with the John Birch Society, Rehnquist picked up

an unexpected ally from one of the Senate's leading liberals, Senator Edward Kennedy. On hearing these remarks by Rauh concerning Rehnquist's associations, Kennedy snapped, "Your suggestion is completely unwarranted and uncalled for." Kennedy said he had talked with Rehnquist on the subject and had been "completely satisfied." Kennedy acknowledged that he, too, had qualms concerning Rehnquist's philosophy but told Rauh, "You ought to have a good deal more evidence before making such statements in view of the rather 'poisonous' atmosphere surrounding the controversy."[27]

This interchange is interesting not only for revealing an unusual source of support for Rehnquist but also as a rarity in the long alliance between Senator Kennedy and the Leadership Conference, a national organization of 127 labor, religious, and civil rights groups that had long lobbied for civil rights legislation and that had vigorously opposed President Nixon's two recently defeated high-court nominees. It would be a mistake to draw any inference from this brief spat, as Senator Kennedy's subsequent polite questioning of Rauh demonstrated. Moreover, the senator drew from Rauh the opinion that Rehnquist "didn't just work as a quiet drone" under Attorney General John N. Mitchell but was a fully responsible participant in shaping the Nixon administration's civil rights and civil liberties policies.

There was one overriding question in the minds of many concerning Rehnquist at the time of his nomination, and that was, How many of the highly controversial views he had argued so forcefully during his stint in the Justice Department had been initiated by him and how many had flowered in the minds of President Nixon and Attorney General Mitchell, so that he was simply compelled to present them in the best manner possible in his role as an advocate for those officials? People like Rauh and others in the Leadership Conference were convinced that he was a full-fledged and responsible participant in shaping the civil liberties and civil rights programs of the Nixon administration.

Indeed, Rehnquist's own writings give credence to the

notion that there were few if any differences between the views of President Nixon and those of the nominee. He had previously discussed this subject in print when he explained: "The plain fact of the matter is that any President, and any Attorney General, wants his immediate underlings to be not only competent attorneys, but to be politically and philosophically attuned to the policies of the Administration. This is not peculiar to the Department of Justice, but is a common feature in the staffing of virtually all of the Cabinet departments in the Executive branch of the Government."[28]

One academic, spending a brief sabbatical in the Justice Department during this period, said privately, however, that Rehnquist had received a "bad rap" during this time. As he saw it, Rehnquist was chosen by the department to be its and the president's spokesman for their most extreme or controversial proposals because of his articulateness, his coolness under fire, and his ability as a first-rate legal scholar to think on his feet. Rehnquist was, according to this view, the "point man" for the administration when it faced its most hostile fire.

During the confirmation hearings some evidence did emerge that suggested that the nominee, at least in the past, had not necessarily agreed with various aspects of President Nixon's policies on race relations. On 22 November 1971 Senator Bayh, in the course of the hearings, introduced evidence that he said showed that Rehnquist continued to display an unwillingness to permit the law to be used to promote racial equality in America. According to Bayh, the transcript of the 1966 meeting of the Commissioners on Uniform State Law, at which Rehnquist represented Arizona, showed that he opposed a measure against real estate "blockbusting" and moved to delete a proposal to cope with racial imbalance in employment. The nominee's opposition to a section aimed at helping employers voluntarily cure racial imbalance casts doubt on his claim that he supported the Nixon administration's Philadelphia plan, which had a similar objective, Bayh said. Bayh quoted Rehnquist as telling the conference in 1966 that an antiblockbusting section raised "a constitutional question and a serious policy question, and in view of the combination of these two factors, plus the fact that it doesn't strike me this is a vital part of your bill at all . . . I think this would be a good thing to leave out."[29]

The Justice Department rushed to support the nominee by pointing out that the Arizona delegation had voted unanimously to support final approval of a model civil rights act for the states. In addition, the department pointed to a 5 November 1971 letter from Albert Jenner, Jr., a Chicago lawyer and immediate past chairman of the uniform law conference. Jenner, who, according to the *Washington Post,* was a widely known member of the bar and a supporter of civil rights, wrote that while he disagreed with Rehnquist on policy matters, he found him able and qualified for the Court. Contacted by the *Post* at his office, Jenner said that Rehnquist had led a move at the 1966 conference meeting to have the rights proposal adopted as a model act rather than a uniform act. [30]

That the debate over the "real Rehnquist" was not restricted to the halls of Congress is indicated by a lengthy letter to the *Washington Post* by Richard K. Berg, a former Justice Department lawyer and one who professed to differ considerably with Rehnquist's political and social views. Berg's letter, which appeared in the 9 December 1971 edition, said:

> Since the public discussion of the nomination of Rehnquist to the Supreme Court has turned to a considerable extent on his civil rights record, I believe that some comments of mine may be pertinent.
>
> I served as an attorney in the Office of Legal Counsel of the Department of Justice for eight years (1961–65, 1967–71). In the later period, which included two years under Mr. Rehnquist, I worked on most of the civil rights problems handled by the Office, including the question of the legality of the Philadelphia plan.
>
> Mr. Rehnquist's approach to these problems, like his approach to all other matters on which we worked together, was objective and lawyerlike in the highest degree. He never expressed or showed, to my knowledge,

any reluctance or disinclination to interpret or enforce the laws against discrimination in accordance with a sympathetic reading of their terms. Indeed, the legal opinions and memoranda on civil rights matters issued by the Office during Rehnquist's tenure differed little, if at all, in general philosophy from those issued by his predecessors.

It was suggested, however, in Professor Arthur Miller's article of some weeks ago that Mr. Rehnquist's legal conclusions as head of the Office of Legal Counsel were shaped by a desire to please his superiors. No lawyer can be oblivious to the needs of his client, and the President's lawyer's lawyer is no exception. For any head of the Office there is an obvious tension between his role as adviser to and advocate for the Executive Branch and his role as the foremost interpreter and expounder of the law to the Executive Branch. I served in the office under four assistant attorneys general, all lawyers of uncommon ability and integrity. Of the four, Rehnquist was, in my opinion, the most objective, and the most rigorous in excluding nonlegal considerations from the process of resolving a legal problem.

In his tenure as head of the Office of Legal Counsel, Rehnquist has won the respect and high regard of his colleagues, including many, like myself, whose views on political and social issues differ considerably from his, I believe that Rehnquist is highly qualified for service on the Supreme Court and that the Senate should confirm his nomination. . . . Richard K. Berg (Arlington)

In an editorial on 28 November 1971, the *Washington Post* saw things in a somewhat different light. As it looked at Mr. Rehnquist's past views, the *Post* saw three striking themes running through most of his writings and speeches during the previous fifteen years. These were, as the *Post* saw it, (1) his lack of understanding of the problem of racial discrimination as late as 1964, (2) a somewhat cavalier attitude toward interpretations of the Bill of Rights that differ from his own, and (3) an underlying philosophy about the role of government that runs through so much of what he had to say on these subjects.

Of the three, Mr. Rehnquist's attitude toward civil rights was, in the *Post*'s view, the least troubling. The paper acknowledged that he did oppose a public accommodations law in 1964 and attempted to explain away his action on the grounds that he did not understand "the strong concern that minorities have for the recognition" of their rights. The *Post* wondered, it said, "where he was during the years preceding 1964 when the depth of feeling about such matters was driven home so eloquently by Dr. King and others. But we accept his current statement that his horizons have broadened since then. Perhaps they will broaden more, beyond this. However, the area of civil rights is not one in which his presence on the court is likely to make much difference one way or the other. Its course in that area seems well nigh irreversible."

The second aspect of Rehnquist's views that bothered the *Post* concerned the degree of sensitivity he had shown toward the concepts underlying the Bill of Rights. As the paper reviewed his record, it found it possible to come away with the feeling that Rehnquist thought that those on the other side of the constitutional argument were "almost by definition, Communists, criminals and pornographers." But, it went on, it is also possible to come away with the feeling that "he has merely expressed his position strongly, and perhaps was carried away in his rhetoric by the zest of the struggle." Therefore the paper concluded that in the second area of concern it was inclined to give him the benefit of the doubt, "based principally on the testimony of some of those who have known him well, that he is thoughtful and careful in his approach to constitutional questions."

It was in the third area that the *Post* was most troubled by the past expression of his theories. In its view, the philosophy that tied his speeches and writings together was one "in which property rights outrank human rights and in which the power of government to trample on the civil liberties— free speech, privacy, peaceful protest and the rest—of its citizens outranks the restrictions placed on this power by the Bill of Rights." As the paper perceived Rehnquist's philosophy, "a store owner's desire to select his customers out-weighs a cutomer's desire to be served there; the govern-ment's interest in collecting information is more important than an individual's interest in being free from surveillance; the majority's interest in suppressing pornography or in con-victing criminals far outweighs the individual's rights to read or to be safe from self-incrimination, and so on." This, the *Post* emphasized, is "a view of the Constitution we do not share. But it is the view Mr. Nixon shares and is the view he said he will try to make dominant on the Supreme Court."

Then, in what was to prove a most accurate prediction of Supreme Court voting behavior in the 1980s, the editorial concluded that

> a vote to confirm Mr. Rehnquist is a vote to take a consid-erable risk with the future of civil liberties in this coun-try. It is not as if Mr. Rehnquist would become the first, the second, or the third justice holding his point of view. The breaks of history have given President Nixon a chance to achieve his goal of changing the court's direc-tion with four nominations within the first three years of his term, an opportunity provided only two other Presi-dents—Taft and Harding—since the Civil War. Nor is there compelling evidence that Rehnquist is a flexible and moderate man who might or might not help the President reach his goal. On the contrary, on the basis of his record of articulate commitment, it would seem that his might well become the vote and the voice that tipped the balance. Those senators who believe as we do, that the preservation of vital, court-defined civil liberties is the principal issue at stake here, have in our opinion good and sufficient reason to vote against the confirma-tion of Mr. Rehnquist.[31]

Concerns similar to those voiced by the *Washington Post* failed to persuade a substantial majority of the Senate Judi-ciary Committee. On 30 November 1971 a twelve-member majority overrode the strenuous objections of four Democratic members and reported Rehnquist's nomination to the Senate floor with a forty-page brief in his favor.

In a forty-two-page minority report, Senators Gary Hart, Birch Bayh, Edward Kennedy, and John Tunney charged that Mr. Rehnquist was "outside the mainstream of American thought" on civil rights. They pointed out that "just four years ago" he had opposed the nation's basic goals of racial equality. They also assailed him for what they regarded as a lack of cooperation during the hearing and insensitivity to the rights of citizens, including government employees. They also said that statements like Rehnquist's 1967 comments on school integration in Phoenix—that "we are no more dedicated to an 'integrated society' than we are to a 'segregated society' "—clearly placed him out of step with the American trend toward equal opportunity for all races. The committee's majority report argued that Rehnquist saw both sides of civil liberties issues. The dissenters, however, charged that he consistently gave an exalted value to government power and a low value to individual freedom on issues of wiretapping, government surveillance, free speech, and privacy. In his writing and speeches, the critics said, Rehnquist "consistently dismisses" constitutional claims of individuals while according "the most painstaking and sympathetic analysis to claims for increased government power."[32]

From the outset, the ideological portrait of Justice Rehnquist which emerges—drawn from statements he made while in the Justice Department, in various law review articles, and in testimony before congressional committees—is one that some might see as that of an authoritarian activist. Once on the Court, this is reflected in his consistent stance that when conflicts arise between government authority and individual rights, the government must always prevail. In this sense, Rehnquist is a native example of de Tocqueville's thesis that in America, "lawyers value legality more than freedom, are not altogether averse to tyranny," and "provided the legislature undertakes of itself to deprive men of their independence, are not dissatisfied."[33]

There are three themes running through most of

Rehnquist's writings and speeches prior to his coming to the Court which have troubled civil libertarians then and now. The *Washington Post* summarized these concerns as (1) his lack of understanding of the problems of racial discrimination as late as 1964, (2) a cavalier attitude toward interpretations of the Bill of Rights that differed from his own, and (3) an underlying philosophy about the role of government authority over human rights. The *Post* was willing to accept his more recent statements that his horizons had broadened in the area of race relations. His strident attacks on those on the other side of constitutional issues as "almost by definition Communists, criminals and pornographers," the paper was willing to set aside as hyperbole—as a result of his being "carried away in his rhetoric by the zest of the struggle."

But the *Post* and many legal scholars were deeply troubled by the third theme consistently running through his speeches and writings. This was the continuing refrain "in which property rights outrank human rights and in which the power of government to trample on the civil liberties—free speech, privacy, peaceful protest and the rest—of its citizens outranks the restrictions placed on that power by the Bill of Rights." This view was shared by President Nixon, the paper said, and it was a view that the president was attempting to make dominant on the Court.[34] It was because of this philosophy in particular that the *Post* and others opposed the nomination.

5
Early Racial Views

THE announcement of William Rehnquist's nomination did nothing to warm the hearts of civil rights champions. The *New York Times* reported that many Arizona blacks considered Rehnquist to be a racist. One reason for black reaction was the fact that in 1968 Rehnquist had been an outspoken opponent of a civil rights bill pending before the Arizona legislature.[1]

Shortly after the nomination announcement, Rev. George B. Brooks, a leader in the Arizona NAACP, said that Rehnquist, "was the only major person of stature in the state who opposed the Arizona civil rights bill in 1968." In addition, State Senator Clovis Campbell, a black, said that Rehnquist was a "John Bircher." Moreover, the Arizona chapter of the NAACP, in a meeting in Phoenix on the weekend of 20 September 1971, adopted a resolution opposing Rehnquist's confirmation. At that time, Billie Mills, the Phoenix NAACP president, said, "The opposition is growing because of his strong leanings toward the John Birch Society and other right-wing groups and his stand on the Arizona civil rights legislation." State Senator Campbell said that if Rehnquist were confirmed, "all the good work that has been accomplished by the Supreme Court would be thrown out the window." According to the *New York Times,* in 1969, when Rehnquist was being considered for the position of assistant attorney general, Brooks filed a protest against him with Attorney General John Mitchell. Interestingly enough, Rehnquist was not questioned about this in his public appearance before the Senate Judiciary Committee.

In response to the statements by Arizona blacks, almost all of Rehnquist's former law partners came forward to deny that he was a racist or a member of the John Birch Society. They said that Rehnquist had opposed some civil rights legislation because he considered the proposals to be unconstitutional. On 27 September 1971 the Arizona Bar Association unanimously endorsed the nomination and called for his confirmation by the Senate.[2]

The next step in the drama occurred on 29 September 1971, when the Justice Department made public three documents—two letters to the editor of the *Arizona Republic* and the transcript of Rehnquist's testimony before the Phoenix City Council on 15 June 1964—in which Rehnquist supported de facto segregation and opposed a public accommodations law for Phoenix. Release of these documents to the Senate Judiciary Committee coincided with a meeting of the Leadership Conference on Civil Rights, which, according to the *Washington Post,* also possessed the documents.[3]

In his 9 September 1967 letter to the editor of the *Arizona Republic,* Rehnquist said, "We are no more dedicated to an 'integrated society' than we are to a 'segregated society.' We [are] instead dedicated to a free society, in which each man is accorded the maximum amount of freedom of choice in his individual activities." The documents also revealed that three years before he had opposed the integration plan for Phoenix high schools, Rehnquist had contended that "a measure of our traditional freedom would be lost" if a public accomodations law were enacted for Phoenix. In his 24 June 1964 letter, Rehnquist said that a public accommodations law would not correct the source of indignity to the Negro, but that it would result in "the unwanted customer and the disliked proprietor . . . glowering at one another across the lunch counter." He also argued that the "founders of this nation thought of it as 'the land of the free' just as surely as they thought of it as the land of the equal." To tell a businessman how he must select his customers, said Rehnquist, was to interfere with his freedom to manage his own affairs.[4]

Rehnquist's letter on school integration followed a series of newspaper articles decrying de facto segregation and questioning the value of the traditional neighborhood schools. "The neighborhood school concept," said Rehnquist, works well, and "those who would abandon it, concern themselves not with the great majority . . . but with a small minority for whom they claim it has not worked well. . . . [The minority] may in many cases not even want the privileges." He went on to say that the school's job is to educate children, and schools should not "be saddled with a task of fostering change which may well lessen their ability to perform their primary job."[5]

On the same day that the Justice Department released the documents, Roy Wilkins, executive director of the NAACP, told the Virginia conference of the NAACP that Rehnquist "offers a dangerous future for you" as a Supreme Court justice because "he may not be able to see you for law and order." He went on to say that William Rehnquist "may accept you as a buddy, but his philosophy will kill you." Negro Americans, Wilkins said, "are just as law-abiding as anybody else," but "they believe law and order should not be used as a cloak" for racial discrimination.[6]

Rehnquist also picked up some curiously mixed support from a political adversary in Phoenix, according to the 1 November 1971 issue of the *Washington Post*. John P. Frank, "a leading constitutional and Supreme Court expert" in Phoenix who, according to the *Post*, was a Democrat and had "seen all sides of Rehnquist and his family since they moved to Phoenix in the mid-1950s." This was his appraisal:

> If I were to divide the categories (or criteria for Supreme Court candidates) in terms of legal ability, he is simply top notch. His character is absolutely unimpeachable. He is a thorough gentleman. I have no serious doubts that he should be confirmed. . . . On the other hand, given my premises, he is enough of an extreme conservative that it is a deplorable appointment. He will represent the Goldwater view on the Supreme Court. Bill has been an

77

intellectual force for reaction. I do not believe he will put the manacles back on the slaves, but I'm sure from his point of view it will be more than a pause. . . . there will be a backward movement. In terms of race relations, I would expect him to be retrograde. He honestly doesn't believe in civil rights and will oppose them. On criminal matters he will be a supporter of police methods, in the extreme. On free speech, Bill will be restrictive. On loyalty programs, i.e., McCarthyism, he'll be 100 percent in favor.

But by the normal standards of Supreme Court appointments, Frank said unequivocally that "Rehnquist is entitled to be confirmed, regardless of his philosophy."[7]

On the other hand, Joseph Rauh, Vice-Chairman of Americans for Democratic Action, said on 29 October 1971 that anyone who could take the position Rehnquist did on integration thirteen years after *Brown* v. *Board of Education* "shouldn't be on the Supreme Court."[8]

As the Rehnquist confirmation hearings got under way, the first item introduced was a 2 November 1971 report of the Standing Committee on the Federal Judiciary of the American Bar Association on the nominee's credentials and qualifications. At the outset the report emphasized that the committee had limited its conclusions to the professional competence, judicial temperament, and integrity of the nominee. Without these characteristics, the report said, "no person is qualified to become a Justice of the Supreme Court." The committee recognized that a selection process that involved the president and the Senate also incorporated factors of a broad "political and ideological nature." But since the committee did not take these factors into account, it emphasized that it expressed no opinion on them, "even though, as it will appear from what follows, its investigation revealed opposition from several sources to this nomination on that score." It went on to say that while it "respects opinions on these factors on both sides, it does not attempt to evaluate them, except to the extent, if any, that they appear to affect the element of judicial temperament."

The report went on to say that "limited to the area described above . . . Mr. Rehnquist meets high standards of professional competence, judicial temperament, and integrity. To the committee, this means that from the viewpoint of professional qualifications, Mr. Rehnquist is one of the best persons available for appointment to the Supreme Court." The nine-member committee, however, while unanimous in the view that Rehnquist was qualified for the appointment, had three members who believed that his qualifications did not establish his eligibility for the committee's highest rating, and it thus expressed their conclusion as "not opposed to his confirmation."

The ABA committee also reviewed his academic record and noted that a classmate of Rehnquist's who had been asked to interview members of his Stanford Law School class reported that in their judgment, "Mr. Rehnquist is of exceptional intellectual and legal ability." Moreover, it was noted that while various of the interviewees disagreed with "some of the political and social views of Mr. Rehnquist, each of us is completely satisfied that he will approach his task with objectivity."

To ascertain the nominee's reputation, the committee interviewed more than 120 judges and lawyers in seven states. Among other things it found that "those devoted to expanding concepts of civil rights regret his nomination." On the other hand, it also noted that "a number of leading liberal and civil rights lawyers support the nomination because of his professional competence, intellectual ability, and character." The committee quoted one member of this group who said of Rehnquist that he is "not a Bircher, not a racist, but a decent man and a good human being." One judge who on balance supported his appointment nonetheless had reservations as to his judicial temperament because "Mr. Rehnquist had such deep convictions on social and economic problems that he might be unduly and injudiciously influenced by those views in deciding cases."

Among the law school deans interviewed, all recognized the high quality of Rehnquist's scholarship, although some who knew him only by reputation believed that he might be "so far out of the main stream" with respect to human rights that "his qualifications were questionable." The ABA committee noted that one professor active in the civil rights movement had said that "Mr. Rehnquist lacked the temperament of a Supreme Court Justice, that he was totally ruthless and in that sense lacked integrity." He went on to say that he felt that Rehnquist "was gifted in his ability to make persuasive arguments, but that he was not intellectually honest in making some of them."

In summarizing the views of the academic community, the committee observed that of the sixty-one law schools surveyed, "no dean, and as far as we know, no faculty member has cast doubt as to Mr. Rehnquist's brilliant intellectual qualifications. Our impression from our survey is that a strong preponderance of this group favors his confirmation, notwithstanding sharp opposition to many of his philosophical views."[9]

Russell Baker, in his *New York Times* column of 17 September 1986, during the hearings on Rehnquist's nomination to be chief justice, commented sardonically about the almost mandatory use of the word "brilliant" when referring to the justice. Even his most "vigorous opponents are unable to start flailing away without first remarking that he is 'brilliant' or conceding that his 'brilliance' is undeniable," said Baker. He went on to say, however, that " 'brilliant' is one of Washington's most freely bestowed compliments, probably because it has so many meanings in that inscrutable culture that it may mean almost anything, which is the same as meaning nothing at all." When considering its application to Justice Rehnquist, Baker notes, it is clearly meant as a judgment on his legal career, but "what is truly remarkable about [Rehnquist's] career is its consistency. His judicial opinions are almost as predictable as the arrival of the solstice and equinox."

Justice Rehnquist's mind, explained Baker, "seems to remain almost precisely where it was when he arrived on the Court 15 years ago. He gives every impression of a man who settled upon a philosophy as a youth in law school and has not altered it in any interesting way since." There is a real danger in this approach, Baker suggested. "The mind that never changes is more likely to be calcified than brilliant, at least in the conventional sense of what constitutes brilliance." The word "brilliance" as it is normally used, Baker said, suggests a "showy ability to improvise ingenious solutions when confronted by unforeseeable difficulty."

If our society really cared about the careful use of words, Baker explained, "Justice Rehnquist's 'consistency' rather than his 'brilliance' would be the word on every tongue." But the word "consistency" had little attraction in a city such as Washington, D.C., "perhaps because it is a quality not much admired in a city where people must trim their minds regularly to take advantage of the prevailing wind."

Another problem would arise should the term "consistency" be applied to Rehnquist in place of the word "brilliance," as Baker explained. Critics would be prompted "to recall Emerson's observation that 'a foolish consistency is the hobgoblin of little minds' and that 'With consistency a great soul has simply nothing to do.' 'Brilliance' has no such booby traps." That word, however, and its closely related cousin, "brightest," did fall from favor following the Kennedy administration after David Halberstam's acidly titled work *The Best and the Brightest* presented the history of the men who "made Vietnam synonymous with disaster," Baker notes.

Why then is Justice Rehnquist "constantly lathered in 'brilliance'?" Baker asked. "I believe," he said, "it is because that famously hollow compliment was applied to him when he was first nominated to the Court and young enough to bear it. Since he hasn't changed noticeably since then, the press didn't get around to changing his accompanying adjective." This forces Baker to conclude that Rehnquist's "present 'brilliance' results from his perfect 'consistency.' "

In 1971 the ABA rating committee, while acknowledging Rehnquist's "brilliant intellectual qualifications," did recognize, nonetheless, that "a significant minority would oppose his confirmation, not on grounds of professional qualifications, but on broad questions of the political desirability of so conservative an addition to the court." There were, however, a "very small number" who suggested that his reiterated conservative views manifested a defect going to his professional qualifications.

In the field of civil rights and civil liberties, the committee acknowledged that he had drawn criticism for his public defense of various administration acts and recommendations, as well as for the views he expressed before entering government, which manifested an extremely conservative position as to appropriate governmental actions in certain areas of racial and religious discrimination. After reviewing a large number of his statements as a government official, however, the committee concluded that regardless of the merits of the positions he advocated, "it did not appear that his defense of those positions was beyond proper limits of professional advocacy."

Concerning the views Rehnquist espoused before becoming a government official, such as his opposition to proposed local and state legislation forbidding discrimination in places of public accommodation, the committee recognized that "his views were obviously conservative." In the committee's view, however, such views had been "expressed on philosophical grounds and concerned only the merits of pending legislation. When the legislation was enacted, Mr. Rehnquist in no way attempted to frustrate or oppose the enforcement of the law, and he now acknowledges that its successful execution convinces him that his position was probably wrong on the merits."

The ABA group recognized the almost unanimous opposition to the appointment from labor and civil rights organizations, but it took the position that "the reasons advocated for the opposition of these groups . . . lie outside the area with which the Committee is concerned and to which its opinion is confined." The ABA committee report concluded:

As we stated at the outset, our Committee expresses no view whatever as to Mr. Rehnquist's personal and philosophical views. We have concluded that they do not affect his professional qualifications, that is, his professional competence, judicial temperament and integrity. Accordingly, the Committee is unanimous in its view that he is qualified for appointment to the Supreme Court.[10]

The Senate Judiciary Committee hearings on the Rehnquist nomination also make clear that he drew support from a number of eminent legal scholars within the academic community, people such as Jarril F. Kaplan of the Stanford Law School; John B. Harlbut, professor emeritus of the University of Michigan Law School; Thomas E. Kauper, also of Michigan's law school (and who also worked with the nominee in the Justice Department for a time); Robert H. Bork of Yale; Ralph K. Winter, Jr., of the University of Chicago's law school; and Phil C. Neal, lately of Stanford but then dean of the Arizona State University College of Law. Each of these individuals separately wrote to the committee supporting the nomination.

Jarril F. Kaplan, who at one time had served as chairman of the Phoenix Human Relations Commission, noted that "In all my years of intergroup relations in [Phoenix], I never once heard reference to Mr. Rehnquist as bearing hostility toward minority persons." In recalling Rehnquist's opposition to city and state civil rights legislation, Kaplan noted that "unlike others, whose opposition was clearly suspect, Mr. Rehnquist's objections were based on legal grounds which he presented in a sincere fashion . . . [and] it is neither accurate nor fair to label him as a 'racist,' sophisticated or otherwise."

Others, such as Kauper of Michigan and Neal of Arizona, who apparently were aware of expressions of concern over Rehnquist's views on race relations, tended to brush such worries aside summarily. Kauper, for example, indicated that "I have been somewhat dismayed by charges made during the past weeks that he is a 'racist.' That is a term used rather loosely these days, but I surely hope that we have not reached that point where all political conservatives must bear the racist label. Mr. Rehnquist is, of course, on the conservative side of the political spectrum. But I neither saw nor heard anything during my two years in the [Justice] Department which would in any way suggest that Mr. Rehnquist had any tendency toward racism. Charges to the contrary seem wholly unwarranted."

Phil C. Neal, who had taught Rehnquist while at Stanford, said in his letter, "I am confident that he is a fair-minded and objective man. Any suggestions of racism or prejudice are completely inconsistent with my recollections of him."

The statement of enthusiastic support by a future justice of the Supreme Court—Sandra Day O'Connor—found its way into the testimony before the Senate Judiciary Committee at an early stage by being included in the opening remarks by Senator Paul Fannin of Arizona on 3 November 1971. As State Senator O'Connor saw Rehnquist's views on race relations: "When Bill has expressed concern about any law or ordinance in the area of civil rights, it has been to express a concern for the preservation of individual liberties, of which he is a staunch defender in the tradition of the late Justice Black." According to Senator Fannin, O'Connor went on to say that "he has the potential to become one of the greatest jurists of our highest court." She also added that as a law student, "he quickly rose to the top of the class and, frankly, was head and shoulders above all the rest of us in terms of sheer legal talent and ability."[11] Such views may help explain Justice O'Connor's later voting behavior as a member of the Supreme Court, where she has a strong proclivity to side with Justice Rehnquist.

By the time of his confirmation hearings, Rehnquist's views seem to have moderated, at least in the area of race relations. He told the Senate Judiciary Committee that he had "come to realize the strong concern of minorities for the recognition of these rights." He went on to tell the committee that he no longer subscribed to his past criticism of the 1964 ordinance requiring Phoenix business establishments to serve all customers regardless of race.[12]

Senator Birch Bayh quizzed Rehnquist about the letter he had written as a private citizen in 1964 criticizing the recently enacted Phoenix public accommodations ordinance. In the letter Rehnquist had said that the new law "sacrificed owners' property rights and heaped an indignity on them comparable to the prejudice against Negroes." When asked if this was his opinion now, Rehnquist replied, "I think probably not. The ordinance has really worked very well in Phoenix."[13]

He was also asked about his previous opposition to busing to increase school integration and whether his views on this subject had also changed. Rehnquist said he adhered to his previous view with regard to localities that have not been found guilty of operating officially sponsored dual school systems. "My children attend integrated schools with a small number of blacks in nearby Virginia," he said in the context of his attitudes toward neighborhood schools. He went on to say that his son played on football and basketball teams with blacks and said, "I feel he is better off for that experience."[14]

The hearings that day also brought forth other Rehnquist views on race relations. For example, he stood by his opposition to long-distance busing to provide a better school racial mix in Phoenix, but he went on to say, "I am not sure I know enough" about the school situation there to "judge whether drastic measures are needed to equalize educational opportunities." He also said that in his view it was the "proper role for the court" to reexamine in 1954 the half-century-old doctrine of "separate but equal facilities" for blacks and whites.[15]

Representing the Leadership Conference on Civil Rights, Joseph Rauh told the Judiciary Committee that he could not accept Rehnquist's testimony that he had changed his views on the public accommodations law of Phoenix because it worked and because he had come to realize the aspirations of minorities. That amounted to saying, "I hadn't realized the minorities really cared about this," at a time when Congress was struggling to pass a national public accommodations law, Rauh said. Rehnquist "is opposed to the goals of desegregation, not just the means," Rauh said, adding, "He is a man of his convictions, wrong as they are."[16]

During this stage of the hearings, charges were made that in the early 1960s Rehnquist had intimidated black and Hispanic voters at a polling place in Phoenix, where he was then a local Republican activist. His main line of attack, it was said, was to challenge potential black or Hispanic voters on the grounds of their inability to read. Until 1964 it was legal in Arizona to challenge a person's right to vote on the grounds of illiteracy. The allegations were apparently nettling enough so that Rehnquist felt constrained to write a letter to the Senate after the confirmation hearings were over but before the full Senate had acted. In the letter he flatly denied the charge, stating categorically that he had not "personally engaged in challenging the credentials of any voter."[17]

This was a charge, however, that would not die. It arose again to haunt Justice Rehnquist during the Senate Judiciary Committee hearings on his nomination to be chief justice in 1986. This time the impact seemed to be more damaging. In the most recent hearings he was more circumspect in asserting his role as an activist than he had been in 1971. In the latest hearing he claimed that his function on Election Day was to provide legal advice to Republicans assigned the task of challenging voters' credentials. Then, as *Time* magazine put it, "peppering his testimony with 'I don't recalls,' he said he did not believe he had ever challenged any voters."[18]

As the 1986 hearings proceeded, however, a far less benevolent picture of his activities emerged from the testimony of four witnesses who had not participated in the 1971 Senate procedures. For example, psychology professor Sydney Smith, a Democratic poll watcher at the time, said that in the 1960s he had seen Rehnquist go up to two black men at the polls and say to them, "You're not able to read, are you? You have no business being here."

Another person challenging Rehnquist's version who testified in the 1986 hearings was San Francisco attorney

James Brosnahan, who had been an assistant United States attorney in Phoenix in 1962. Brosnahan specifically contradicted Rehnquist's sworn testimony. He recalled that he had been summoned by panicky voters and officials to a precinct where Rehnquist was a challenger, and he told the committee he assumed that it was Rehnquist's "blanket" challenges of black and Hispanic voters that had led to the tense situation, although he had not personally seen Rehnquist challenge anyone. Nonetheless, he testified that Rehnquist's conduct "was designed to reduce the number of black and Hispanic voters by confrontation and intimidation."[19]

Curiously enough, at this stage in the 1986 hearings Victor Maggiore, who in the early 1960s had been the chairman of the Phoenix-area Democratic party, claimed he had never heard any negative reports about Rehnquist's Election Day activities and, he insisted, "All of these things would have come through me."[20]

Another sidelight of the 1986 hearings was the testimony concerning the FBI's discovery that Rehnquist had bought two houses that were subject to discriminatory deed restrictions. His current summer home in Greensboro, Vermont, purchased in 1974, includes a clause barring sale of the house to "anyone of the Hebrew race." Perhaps of more significance was the fact that the restrictive clause was not part of the standard printed document but had been typed in specifically.

Justice Rehnquist at first told the Senate committee he had only recently become aware of the restriction's existence.[21] One week later, however, he acknowledged that his lawyer had, in fact, sent him a letter in 1974 informing him that the deed barred its transfer to members of the Hebrew race. He then said, "I did not recall the letter or its contents before I testified last week." Rehnquist testified that he found the restriction "obnoxious" and that it was unenforceable under the 1948 *Shelly* v. *Kramer* Supreme Court ruling.[22]

Next it was disclosed that Rehnquist had once owned another home in Phoenix and that its deed had included a restrictive covenant prohibiting transfer to anyone not of the

"Caucasian race." The justice could not recall having seen the deed, which he had, in fact, never signed. Responding to sharp questioning by Senator Kennedy, Rehnquist characterized the terms of the deed as "very offensive."[23]

On the day following Rauh's critical testimony in 1971, Senator James O. Eastland had sharply attacked both Rauh and Clarence Mitchell of the Leadership Conference on Civil Rights. In a twenty-page memorandum to supplement the record of Rehnquist's confirmation hearings, Senator Eastland accused the two civil rights leaders of "the crassest type of character assassination" and went on to say that they clearly had gone outside of "the bounds of propriety" in their attacks on Rehnquist. Senator Eastland charged that Rauh and Mitchell had made "highly misleading and unfairly prejudicial" statements about Rehnquist when they had testified against him the day before.[24]

The Eastland memorandum also noted the charges made by the civil rights spokesmen to the effect that Rehnquist had harassed black voters in Phoenix, berated a black political leader, opposed the goal of integration, and made extreme statements hostile to civil rights and civil liberties. Actually, said Eastland, there was no credible evidence that Rehnquist had shown hostility to Negroes in Arizona, and his views were "far more moderate" than his opponents claimed. Moreover, the senator said, Rauh had unfairly sought to discredit Rehnquist's sworn affidavit that he had never belonged to the John Birch Society when Rauh "insinuated" that the denial left room for "some connection" with the right-wing organization.[25]

His colleague's lengthy memorandum failed to convince Senator Edward Brooke of Massachusetts, the one black in the United States Senate. On 2 December 1971 Brooke said he would vote against the confirmation because of Rehnquist's racial views. "I have always been dedicated to the concept of an integrated society," he said. "I have opposed black separatists and white separatists alike in their efforts to divide the races of man." Therefore, Senator Brooke went on, "After a thorough review of the record and after a thorough study of this particular case, I have regrettably reached the conclusion that I cannot vote for Mr. Rehnquist's confirmation.''[26] Amplifying on his position in a conversation with reporters, Brooke said he had made his decision on Rehnquist's overall record but was particularly disturbed by a letter the nominee had written to the *Arizona Republic* in 1967 opposing a school desegregation plan.

Other elements of Rehnquist's testimony and background continued to trouble civil rights leaders. Some are reflected in a letter to the editor of the *Washington Post* on 4 December 1971 written by Joseph Rauh and Clarence Mitchell. The lengthy letter said in part:

> Over the years, there has been only one area of civil rights legislation where conservatives, liberals and even some of the Deep South members of the Senate and House could reach agreement. That is the right to vote. Thus, because of his personal and organizational involvement in denying Negroes the right to vote in Arizona, Mr. Rehnquist is out of step even with many segregationists who welcome voting by colored Americans.
>
> Mr. Rehnquist's participation in attempts to bar voters from casting their ballots took two forms. First, he personally was present in some precincts when unconscionable attempts were made to prevent elderly and timid black citizens from voting. He says he was there to halt abuses by others. In contradiction there are witnesses who have signed sworn affidavits alleging that it was Mr. Rehnquist, himself, who was interfering with the voters. Neither the White House nor the United States Department of Justice has dared to let Mr. Rehnquist return to the Senate Judiciary Committee to answer these charges in person. . . .
>
> The second aspect of the Rehnquist operation on voting is very troublesome. It will be remembered that in 1964 the Congress passed a law prohibiting the giving of oral literacy tests, unless the Attorney General gave a special extension. Even the Rehnquist supporters admit his role in asking them to read or recite parts of the United States Constitution. This campaign was so well organized, so widespread and so obstructive that one ob-

server of what was going on said, "It is a wonder someone didn't get killed."

Mr. Rehnquist's role in this campaign has been given
various descriptions. Sometimes he is pictured as the
benign lawyer who was opposed to what was happening.
Sometimes he is cast in the part of a relief man who
dropped in to the polling places to give others a rest period. One report credited him with being in charge of
"ballot security." Whatever may have been his rank or
serial number, one thing is clear: He was deeply involved
in a scheme which, on its face, seems to have been a
violation of federal law. . . .

The public has a right to know just what Mr.
Rehnquist was doing. Did he get the program started?
Did he advise the troops that trying to make would-be
voters pass oral literacy tests was illegal? Did he sanction
the sending of letters warning people that they might get
arrested for voting? These and many other questions
have not been answered in an open hearing.[27]

That there was at least some justification for the fears
echoed in the Rauh-Mitchell letter can be seen in an earlier
New York Times story quoting a variety of Rehnquist's writings. On the subject of the mandatory transportation of pupils to achieve integration in schools, Rehnquist had written
some years before in the *Arizona Law Review:* "The question of the extent to which mandatory transportation of pupils is required to achieve 'integration' in school districts
where de jure segregation at one time obtained is a large open
one under existing decisions of the Supreme Court. Clearly
there is nothing in the language of the Constitution itself
which can be said to impose such requirements. In this situation, the Department of Justice is in no sense legally required
to support the imposition of segregation plans containing
massive busing requirements."[28]

What was not known to the Senate or the media at the
time of the hearings but which surfaced several months later
is the fact that Rehnquist, at the request of the White House,

had written both a draft and a detailed justification for a constitutional amendment barring busing to achieve racial balance in the public schools. The effect of the amendment,
which had been proposed in 1970 while Mr. Rehnquist was a
member of the Justice Department and which was contained
in two memorandums that were obtained by the *New York
Times* in 1972, would have been to prevent any sort of formal
busing to achieve racial balance in a given school district.[29] In
a concession that many conservative busing opponents have
since made, however, the proposal would have permitted
what has become known as "freedom of choice"—pupils voluntarily choosing to be bused to other schools within their
districts, even if their motives were racial.

According to the *Times*, White House aides were closely
involved in the two Rehnquist memorandums dated 3 and 5
March 1970. The request, the aides said, went to various departments and specialists, particularly at the Justice Department and the Department of Health, Education and Welfare,
for their "thinking" on the entire question of busing, and the
replies were intended to be fed into the debate then going on
within the administration. The president subsequently decided to postpone any decision on the question, but in later
administration discussions leading up to the president's
speech on the subject on 16 March 1972, White House
sources said, the thinking represented in the Rehnquist
memorandums was very much alive. Nonetheless, the president did propose legislation, instead of a constitutional
amendment, to prohibit further mandatory busing.

Despite his activities in this area, since taking his place
on the bench Rehnquist had not avoided taking part in decisions on busing cases or the Court's role in achieving school
desegregation, the *Times* pointed out. Furthermore, he did
not wish to comment on his earlier memorandums when
contacted by the paper on 16 March 1972.

In the two memorandums Rehnquist said that a constitutional amendment would resolve many of the difficulties inherent in antibusing legislation because legislation would
tempt each subsequent session of Congress to reopen the en-

tire debate and raise the possibility of a multiplicity of conflicting interpretations in the lower federal courts. In addition
to permitting the "freedom of choice" option, the proposed
Rehnquist amendment would also have explicitly prohibited
school districts from denying this choice to blacks or any
groups of pupils except on the grounds of school capacity,
unavailability of transportation, or other "nonracial considerations." In most districts, however, the paper explained, this
was a moot point, because white parents who had fought
busing would be little inclined to submit voluntarily, and
black parents had often found themselves confronted with
packed schools when they sought to initiate transfer for their
children.

Much of the text of the detailed memorandums consisted
of a justification of why neighborhood schools should be pre-
served and legalized under the Constitution and why
"freedom of choice" should be permitted in any effort to
break enforced segregation in some areas of the South by the
voluntary actions of parents and pupils. As Mr. Rehnquist
put it in the memorandums:

> The words, "freedom of choice" and "neighborhood
> schools" do not arise in a vacuum but arise instead in a
> contest of more than 15 years of litigation over what the
> Constitution does and does not permit local school
> boards to do when those boards deal with radically
> mixed student populations.
>
> The critical issue in the South now, which has in the
> past, of course, had in its schools a system of enforced
> segregation, by race, appears to be the "freedom of
> choice" plan, whereunder a student is free to choose to
> attend some school or schools in the district other than
> the one to which he is initially assigned.
>
> In the North, the critical issue (less in public focus at
> the moment than the issue of "freedom of choice" in the
> South) is that of de facto segregation. . . . Does the Con-
> stitution require a school district to take affirmative
> steps to achieve "racial balance" among its schools, even
> though the "balance" existing stems from residential

segregation or other factors for which the school board is not responsible?

In his second memorandum Rehnquist said that the amendment would be drawn so as not to confuse local school boards. He explained:

> If the zoning plan adopted bears a reasonable relationship to educational needs—if fair-minded school board members could have selected it for nonracial reasons—it is valid regardless of the intent with which the particular school boards may have chosen it. The result is to give some certainty to school boards, and not make every zoning attendance plan in a multi-racial school district depend on how the local Federal District judge sizes up the state of mind of the various school board members.

In pressing his case for a constitutional amendment over any form of legislation on the issue, Rehnquist said: "I believe that once the decision has been made [to take some action against school busing] the arguments in favor of doing it by a constitutional amendment heavily preponderate." He went on to say, "Embodiment of the validation in a statute would invite unnecessary detail and would likewise invite frequent reopening of heated debates on the subject." Furthermore, he added, the use of a statute instead of an amendment "has the collateral effect of inserting federal courts still further into the business of operating schools, rather than at least partially withdrawing them from that business."

The constitutional amendment that Rehnquist proposed reads as follows:

> Section 1. No provision of the Constitution shall be construed to prohibit the United States, any state, or any subdivision of either from assigning persons to its educational facilities on the basis of geographic boundaries provided only that such boundaries are reasonably re-

lated to school capacity, availability of transportation, safety or other similar considerations.

Section 2. No provision of the Constitution shall be considered to prohibit the United States, any state, or any subdivision of either from permitting persons to choose or transfer voluntarily among its educational facilities, provided only that the opportunity to choose or transfer is available either to all persons within its jurisdiction or to any eligible person, when standards of eligibility are related to school capacity, availability of transportation, availability of curriculum, safety or other similar considerations.

It is interesting, if idle, to speculate on the reaction of civil rights groups, the media, and Congress had these facts been known during the Rehnquist nomination hearings. For example, would it have proved to be the necessary spark to light the backfire against the Rehnquist appointment that Senator Bayh and other opponents had sought in vain? Or would it merely have been shrugged off by a Senate weary of the continued controversies over President Nixon's Supreme Court appointments?

In summary, the announcement of Rehnquist's nomination to the Supreme Court brought cries of outrage from civil rights groups both within his adopted state of Arizona and throughout the nation. References were made to his consistent opposition to efforts to reduce practices of racial discrimination through law both in the city of Phoenix and in the state of Arizona while he practiced there. These efforts included his opposition to a public accommodations law for Phoenix and the fact that he was the only person of stature to oppose the Arizona civil rights bill of 1968, as well as his open opposition to an integration plan for the Phoenix public high schools in 1964.

The American Bar Association's Standing Committee on the Federal Judiciary, in approving his nomination, limited its conclusions to the nominee's professional competence, judicial temperament, and integrity. It recognized that the presidential selection process incorporated factors of a broad "political and ideological nature," but the committee did not take these into account and expressed no opinion on them. Three of the nine members of the committee did not believe the nominee's qualifications entitled him to the committee's highest rating, though the report found that "Mr. Rehnquist meets high standards of professional competence, judicial temperament, and integrity." The ABA committee, while acknowledging Rehnquist's "brilliant intellectual qualifications," also recognized that a "significant minority would oppose his confirmation, not on grounds of professional qualifications, but on broad questions of the political desirability of so conservative an addition to the Court." Moreover, the committee recognized the almost unanimous opposition to his appointment from labor and civil rights organizations.[30]

The Senate hearings on Rehnquist's nomination produced the information that he stood by his opposition to long-distance busing to provide a better racial mix in Phoenix schools but that his children attended an integrated school in Virginia with a small number of blacks. There were also allegations that in the 1960s Rehnquist had intimidated black and Hispanic voters at a polling place in Phoenix. In the 1971 hearings he flatly denied this. When the charges resurfaced in the 1986 hearings with additional witnesses testifying in support of the charges Rehnquist was more circumspect. Then, as *Time* magazine put it, "peppering his testimony with 'I don't recalls,' he said he did not believe he had ever challenged any voters."[31]

Other 1986 testimony revealed that at different times he had purchased two homes with restrictive racial or religious covenants as part of the deed restrictions. At first Justice Rehnquist told the committee that he had only recently become aware of one restriction's existence, but he later changed his testimony to admit that his attorney had, indeed, informed him in 1974 of the deed's provisions barring transfer to members of "the Hebrew race." He explained, "I did not recall the letter or its contents before I testified last week." Responding to sharp questioning by members of the Senate committee, Rehnquist characterized the terms of the other deed, which prohibited transfer to anyone not of the "Caucasian race," as "very offensive."[32]

Another matter that did not appear in testimony until the 1986 hearings was the fact that Rehnquist, at the request of the Nixon White House, had written both a draft and a detailed justification for a constitutional amendment barring busing to achieve racial balance in the public schools. The Nixon administration later changed its approach to proposing legislation rather than a constitutional amendment to accomplish the same purpose. Despite his deep involvement in the preparation and the support for the Nixon policy of attempting to bar busing, immediately after coming to the Court Rehnquist did not recuse (disqualify) himself from active participation in cases involving issues of busing to attain racial balance.

6

More Controversy
over Race, Theory,
and Procedure

PROBABLY the most stunning revelation of Rehnquist's earlier views on race relations came in the form of a story in *Newsweek* magazine the week of 6 December 1971. The article presented evidence to suggest that he had defended the "separate but equal" doctrine of southern segregationists while he was clerking for Supreme Court Justice Robert Jackson. During the 1952 term of the Court Rehnquist, according to *Newsweek,* wrote a one-and-a-half page, single-spaced legal memorandum on a pending case under the heading, "A Random Thought on the Segregation Cases."

In the memorandum Rehnquist, who was then twenty-eight years old, wrote that the separate-but-equal doctrine laid down by the Supreme Court in *Plessy* v. *Ferguson* in 1896 was right and should be reaffirmed. This was, of course, written two years before the Court overturned the separate-but-equal doctrine in *Brown* v. *Board of Education.* The Rehnquist argument was based on the theory of judicial self-restraint. In this regard, he pointed out that the Court had earlier held that it was not the judicial function "to thwart public opinion except in extreme cases." This principle, he urged, should be applied to the school segregation cases.

"Regardless of the justice's individual views on the merits of segregation," he wrote, "it quite clearly is not one of those extreme cases which commands intervention from one of my conviction." Moreover, he wrote,

> To those who would argue that "personal" rights are more sacrosanct than "property" rights, the short answer is that the Constitution makes no such distinction. To the argument made by Thurgood, not John, Marshall that a majority may not deprive a minority of its constitutional rights, the answer must be made that while this is sound in theory, in the long run it is the majority who will determine what the constitutional rights of the minority are.[1]

Mr. Rehnquist also contended in the 1952 memo that the Court's efforts over the years to protect minority rights had "been sloughed off and crept silently to rest. . . . If the present court is unable to profit by this example, it must be prepared to see its work fade in time, too, as embodying only the sentiments of a transient majority of nine men." After Rehnquist resigned as a clerk for the Court in 1953 and went to practice law in Phoenix, Justice Jackson joined the other members of the Court in unanimously overruling *Plessy* and ordering school desegregation.[2]

It did not take Mr. Rehnquist long to respond to the *Newsweek* story. According to his version, sharply denied by Justice Jackson's longtime secretary, the views expressed in the 1952 memo represented Justice Jackson's thinking, not his own.[3] In a letter to Senate Judiciary Committee chairman James Eastland, Rehnquist said he recalled preparing the memorandum "as a statement of Justice Jackson's tentative views for his own use." According to Rehnquist, these thoughts would then be used by Jackson when conferring with other justices on the pending case, which later became the nation-shaking *Brown* v. *Board of Education* in 1954.

In his letter, Rehnquist disavowed the 1952 memorandum's most provocative statement, which read: "I fully realize that it is an unpopular and unhumanitarian position, for which I have been excoriated by liberal colleagues, but I think *Plessy* v. *Ferguson* was right and should be reaffirmed." Saying he was trying his best to reconstruct an event nineteen years earlier, he went on to call the statement in the 1952 memo a "bald, simplistic conclusion which was not an accurate statement of my own views at the time." Smarting from the attacks during his confirmation hearings concerning his stance on civil rights and civil liberties, Rehnquist concluded his three-page letter to Eastland by stating: "In view of some of the recent Senate floor debate, I wish to state unequivocally that I fully support the legal reasoning and the rightness from the standpoint of fundamental fairness of the *Brown* decision."

Shortly after Senator Eastland made public Rehnquist's letter to him, the Nixon Justice Department was asked whether the memorandum's controversial sentence sounded more like a law clerk writing his own views or preparing remarks for a justice of the Supreme Court. A department spokesman replied that the sentence, despite its use of the first person, was entirely consistent with Rehnquist's own recollection that the views expressed were not his own.[4]

Senator Bayh, one of his critics, in what some viewed as a remarkably mild manner, reacted to Rehnquist's statement that he now supported the 1954 *Brown* decision by saying that he, Bayh, had "some cause to question the veracity of it," since Rehnquist had "ample opportunity" to express such support during his confirmation hearings. Rehnquist responded to this by saying that he was asked only whether he considered the decision a binding precedent.

In a classic case of being damned if you do, and damned if you don't, Rehnquist found himself being criticized by one of his staunchest supporters for writing the letter. Senator Eastland read the letter aloud in the Senate chamber and then said, "I didn't think he should write this letter because the memorandum certainly was what was the law at that time, 1952." Eastland, an outspoken opponent of the *Brown* ruling in 1954, said that Rehnquist had been "badly mistreated," because the memo had been disclosed and discussed with "no attempt to get the facts" behind it, to which Senator Bayh replied that he had been trying to get those facts for three days.[5]

According to the *Washington Post* at the time, opponents of the Rehnquist nomination were contending that the 1952 memorandum was part of the nominee's consistent pattern of hostility to the advancement of minority rights. His supporters, on the other hand, have contended that controversial positions espoused by Rehnquist represent either views he has altered or positions he took as an advocate for the programs of the Nixon administration.

On 9 December 1971 the dispute over the Jackson memo grew more heated when two former employees of the late justice gave the Senate new information on the subject. As a result, an already confused situation became even more confused by the fact that in some respects the information presented by one tended to conflict with that presented by the other. The developments occurred on the eve of a vote scheduled for noon the following day on whether to close off debate on the Rehnquist nomination, thus setting the stage for a showdown vote on his confirmation within a day or two. Both sides were predicting a close vote.

Donald Cronson, an international lawyer and a fellow law clerk at the Court in 1952, cabled the Senate from London that Rehnquist and he had prepared not one but two memorandums for Jackson—one on each side of the school desegregation cases that were pending at that time. In a sense, Cronson corroborated Rehnquist's recollection that a memorandum that bore his initials and that urged reaffirmation of the Court's 1896 separate-but-equal ruling did not reflect Rehnquist's personal views on race relations. Cronson's cable failed, however, to mention Rehnquist's recollection that the views expressed in the memo were those of Justice Jackson and were probably prepared for his personal use in discussing the school desegregation cases at the Court's private conferences.[6]

Cronson's cable said that the controversial memo had been prepared at Jackson's specific request after the justice had examined an earlier memo on which the two law clerks had collaborated. The earlier memo, Cronson explained, called for overruling the 1896 *Plessy* v. *Ferguson* decision but urged that the Court should leave to Congress the responsibility for remedying the effects of a half-century of officially approved segregation. After examining this memo, Jackson had called for a contradicting memorandum arguing that the 1896 case had been correctly decided.

Once again, the cable continued, the two clerks both made contributions. Cronson said that he had contributed at least as much to the pro-segregation memo calling for the breaking of new legal ground as had Rehnquist. In referring to the second memo, the cable said: "A great deal of its contents were the result of my suggestions. A number of phrases . . . I can recognize as having been composed by me and it is probable that the memorandum is more mine than [Rehnquist's]." Cronson said he had examined his files and found that he still had the first memorandum in his possession.[7]

On 10 December 1971 the *Washington Post* interviewed Cronson by telephone from Gstaad, Switzerland. Cronson went beyond his cable to say that in 1952 both Rehnquist and he had arrived at the view that the *Plessy* doctrine was wrong and should be overturned. On the other hand, Cronson, an oil-company lawyer based in London, refused to discuss Jackson's personal views and said he was reluctant to make public his copy of the first memorandum. As he put it, he would not divulge the memo without first talking with Rehnquist—"something I haven't done in 20 years"—and even then he would still have to resolve questions of propriety.[8]

At this time, too, University of Chicago law professor Philip B. Kurland, custodian of the Jackson papers, gave support to Rehnquist's opponents by noting that the Rehnquist explanation of the memo was implausible, both because Jackson had held more liberal views on race relations and because he had not used his research assistants for such chores.[9] Kurland also said that the memo cited by Cronson was not now in the Jackson files in Chicago. He said he had given liberal access to the Jackson papers, including the controversial memo, to scholars during the several years he had been using them for a biography of the justice. Kurland also noted that the files contained a partial draft by Jackson of a 1954 opinion that, if completed and delivered, could have become a concurring opinion to Warren's opinion for the Court in *Brown* v. *Board of Education.*

The other employee who entered the controversy was Elsie Douglas, Justice Jackson's secretary for nine years before his death in 1954. She charged that Rehnquist, by attributing the pro-segregation memorandum's views to Jackson had "smeared the reputation of a great justice." In a telephone interview with the *Washington Post* on 11 December 1971 from her home in a Washington apartment house, Mrs. Douglas also challenged Rehnquist's assertion that Jackson would have asked a law clerk to help prepare the remarks he would make when the nine justices met to decide whether to overturn the separate-but-equal doctrine. According to the *Post,* Mrs. Douglas said the procedure outlined by Cronson was not out of keeping with the practices of many justices over the years. She said, however, that Rehnquist's account was a disservice to a jurist who needed no clerical help to formulate his own arguments to his fellow justices. She went on to recall that Jackson had such a reputation for spontaneous eloquence that the late Justice Felix Frankfurter, for whom she had also worked as a secretary, once proposed that Jackson should be appointed "Solicitor General for life." Indeed, Jackson had been both solicitor general—the government's top courtroom advocate, who argues the major cases before the Supreme Court—and attorney general before his appointment to the high court in 1941, and his orations as chief prosecutor at the post–World War II war crimes trials at Nuremburg are still widely regarded as classics of advocacy.

When looking at the justice's legal philosophy, Mrs. Douglas said, "I don't know anyone in the world who was more for equal protection of the laws than Mr. Jackson." It was inconceivable to her that Jackson's sentiments could have resembled the memo's contention that school segregation was not sufficiently extreme a deprivation of rights to warrant intervention by the courts. She added that her reaction to the Rehnquist contention was "one of shock."[10]

Later evidence also contradicts the Rehnquist contention that the views expressed were those of Justice Jackson. In 1985, as part of the background work for his lengthy interview with Justice Rehnquist, John Jenkins of the *New York Times* discussed the matter with Professor Dennis J. Hutchinson of the University of Chicago, who is Justice Jackson's biographer. Professor Hutchinson, after inspecting all of Justice Jackson's papers from the Court—"every box, every detail"—said he had found no other instance during Jackson's thirteen years on the Court when, as Rehnquist insisted had happened, Jackson had asked a law clerk to prepare a memo for conference discussion summarizing the justice's views.[11]

In the course of his research, however, Hutchinson discovered two additional Rehnquist memos on race relations. In one, Rehnquist endorsed an appeals-court ruling in *Terry* v. *Adams* that effectively denied blacks the right to vote in Texas Democratic Club elections that had determined every countywide race since 1889. (The issue was whether the club was purposefully designed to exclude blacks from voting. Registered white voters were automatically members.)[12]

In the other memo, written after the Court had agreed to hear *Terry* v. *Adams,* Mr. Rehnquist told Justice Jackson:

> The Constitution does not prevent the majority from banding together, nor does it attaint success in the effort. It is about time the Court faced the fact that *the white people in the South don't like the colored people* [emphasis added]; the Constitution restrains them from effecting this dislike through state action, but it most assuredly did not appoint the Court as a sociological watchdog to rear up every time private discrimination raised its admittedly ugly head. To the extent that this decision advances the frontier of state action and "social gain," it pushes back the frontier of freedom of association and majority rule. Liberals should be the first to real-

103

ize, after the past 20 years, that it does not do to push
blindly through toward one constitutional goal without
paying attention to other equally desirable values that
are being trampled on in the process.[13]

It should come as no surprise to anyone familiar with the
Court's history to find that Justice Jackson rejected this
argument and joined seven other justices in finding that
blacks had been unconstitutionally denied voting rights. Of
course, in 1954 he also joined the *Brown* ruling.

At about the same time, Senators Birch Bayh and
Edward Brooke were attacking Rehnquist's version of the
memo's meaning, saying its tone and structure made it impossible for the words to be intended as something Jackson
would adopt as his own. Bayh, in a floor speech, and Brooke,
in remarks inserted into the record, insisted that the law
clerk could not have seriously intended Jackson to criticize
"150 years of attempts on the part of this court to protect
minority rights of any kind—whether those of business,
slaveholders or Jehovah's Witnesses." The latter reference
was to the fact that Jackson had been the author of a famous
1943 Supreme Court opinion vindicating the right of school
children who were Jehovah's Witnesses to refrain from an
otherwise compulsory salute to the flag.[14]

On the same day, Senator Jacob Javits (R-N.Y.) joined
Brooke as the second Republican to speak against Rehnquist.
Senator J. William Fulbright (D-Ark.) also came out against
the nominee and announced his advocacy in congressional
testimony of the supremacy of the executive branch over
Congress.[15]

On the other hand, opponents of Rehnquist's nomination
received a setback when they were unable to dissuade Senator William Proxmire (D-Wis.) from announcing that he
would vote for the forty-seven-year-old assistant attorney
general. Although he differed with Rehnquist's philosophy,
Proxmire said, he respected his intellect and temperament.[16]
Shortly after this, the opposition to the Rehnquist appointment led by Senator Bayh swiftly collapsed, and on 11 December 1971 the Senate confirmed the nominee by a vote of

68 to 26. The four days of Senate debate had won few if any converts to Bayh's position, even though earlier he had spearheaded the defeat of two previous Nixon nominees. Indeed, some observers concluded that the additional debate on the Rehnquist nomination had actually reduced the opposition vote. The final vote found thirty-eight Republicans and thirty Democrats supporting the Rehnquist appointment.[17]

Rehnquist's outspokenly conservative philosophy differed significantly from that of many senators who voted for him, such as Adlai E. Stevenson III (D-Ill.), William Proxmire (D-Wis.), and Charles Mathias (R-Md.). But opponents fell far short of attracting the group of Senate centrists who had made the difference in the 1969 defeat of Clement F. Haynsworth, Jr., and the 1970 rejection of G. Harrold Carswell. The only Republicans voting against confirmation were Edward Brooke (Mass.), Jacob Javits (N.Y.), and Clifford Case (N.J.).[18]

Following the Senate vote, President Nixon emphasized the caliber of both Powell and Rehnquist by saying that "the quality of the court has been enhanced for years to come." He also said that he expected his two new appointees to apply the law without any political consideration. Attorney General Mitchell seemed to second these sentiments by forecasting that these two men would be eminently unpredictable in the way they voted after they took their seats on the Court.

On the other hand, the *Washington Post* editorially pointed out that "the fact that Mr. Nixon finds it necessary to say such obvious things about the independence of the court suggests that down deep inside he is troubled by some of the rhetoric he and some of his supporters were using in talking about the court not so long ago."[19] The *Post* considered Attorney General Mitchell's prediction about the unpredictability of the two new justices to be both more appropriate and more encouraging. It went on to survey a list of presidents who had been disappointed in the judicial decision making of some of their appointments to the Court—such as Theodore Roosevelt with Oliver Wendell Holmes, Woodrow Wilson with

105

James C. McReynolds, and Dwight D. Eisenhower with Earl Warren. "So," the *Post* said, "there is considerable hope for those who cherish civil liberties as we do that the future will not be as drab as it seems, if only Mr. Mitchell's prediction proves true."[20]

There were two major problems, however, with applying historical analogies to the current situation, the paper observed. First, "Mr. Nixon's dream has been fulfilled by his first two nominees in a rather remarkable way. They—Chief Justice Burger and Justice Blackmun—are giving every evidence of being predictable, together, and precisely what the President wanted." Their agreement rate had been so consistent that they had come to be labeled the "Minnesota Twins," the *Post* noted. Particularly in the field of criminal law, they fit closely with what Mr. Nixon said during the 1968 campaign he intended to accomplish. "It is quite clear," the editorial observed, "that if the President has been as prescient in his recent selections as he was in his earlier ones, he had succeeded in turning the court around."[21]

The other fact that caused the *Post* to be skeptical about Attorney General Mitchell's prediction was found in the "unusual posture" of Mr. Rehnquist. He came to the Court possessing a philosophy of constitutional interpretation that was especially well worked out, the paper noted after viewing his writings and speeches. The unpredictability of most justices is traceable to the fact that they have not had time in their busy careers to think about the questions posed by the language of the Constitution. Mr. Rehnquist, the editorial pointed out, "has taken that time and seems to be starting from a base broader than that held by any other new justice in the last 30 years." This should make his actions more predictable. "But," the paper concluded, "maybe Mr. Mitchell knows something the rest of us don't know. We sincerely hope he is right."[22] A history of the justice's opinions written since assuming the bench, clearly demonstrates that the *Post* was correct in suggesting that Rehnquist's opinions would indeed be consistent with the constitutional views he enunciated prior to that time.

It was not long before the trend about which the *Post* was apprehensive began to emerge in the decision making of Justice Rehnquist. As John P. MacKenzie reported less than six months after Rehnquist began his tenure, the Senate Democrats who had tried to drive a wedge between the nominees Powell and Rehnquist could relax, because the two new justices had accomplished a split on their own. As MacKenzie saw it, in a decision handed down on 12 May 1972, "Rehnquist carved out a position of conservatism that made even the soft-spoken former Virginia corporation lawyer look like a liberal. Of the entire court, only Rehnquist held firmly to the view that there was no help in the Constitution for illegitimate children."[23] Powell delivered the opinion of the Court that it was not only unequal, it was "illogical and unjust," to penalize a child for the sins of his parent by denying him rights enjoyed by a child who was born in wedlock. But Rehnquist, in a lone dissent, called into question generations of Supreme Court precedents applying the equal protection clause of the Fourteenth Amendment beyond the realm of race to other forms of discrimination. While all the justices, including Rehnquist, agreed with Powell that it would depart from a 1968 ruling and violate the principle of *stare decisis* if they upheld the Louisiana law, Rehnquist disagreed with that precedent and many others—how many, only time would tell—and argued that the existing precedents were "an extraordinary departure from what I conceive to be the intent of the framers of the Fourteenth Amendment."[24]

The Louisiana law, which was struck down, provided that a worker's legitimate offspring had priority when it came to collecting death benefits. The other dependent children could share in the compensation only if there were enough to go around, and in the case before the Court, there was not. Critics had long condemned such laws as a type of racism, but prior to this case they were handicapped by the fact that on paper the law applied to black and white alike. The Aetna Casualty & Surety Company, defending the state's law, made much of the fact that all the workman's children, legitimate or not, were in this case black. The Louisiana workman had four legitimate children and two born of another woman while his wife was in a mental institution. All the children were part of the man's household.

One month earlier, Rehnquist, also by himself, had dissented from the Court's ruling that a Texas prisoner's suit for equal religious privileges should not have been dismissed out of hand. Condemning what he termed a prison "writ-writer," Rehnquist said that while the Fourteenth Amendment treated racial distinctions as suspect, many of the amendment's framers "would doubtless be surprised to know that convicts came within its ambit."[25]

As MacKenzie pointed out, both utterances had been foreshadowed by Rehnquist's testimony back on 4 November 1971 before the Senate Judiciary Committee when Senator Bayh asked him: "One thing that has troubled me is whether your record can fairly be said to reflect the dedication 'to the great principles of civil rights' of which President Nixon spoke. What have you ever done or said that could help on that concern?" Part of Rehnquist's answer was the statement that "Mr. Justice Miller, I think, made the statement in the 1883 *Slaughterhouse Cases* that in his opinion the principal import of the post–Civil War amendments was to benefit the Negro race." Surprisingly, no senator asked the nominee whether his answer signaled disagreement with the widely accepted notion that the Fourteenth Amendment's guarantee extended to other forms of discrimination.[26]

It will be remembered that during the confirmation battle Senator Bayh had tried without success to portray Rehnquist as dramatically different from Powell. As MacKenzie saw it, "Early signs indicate that the court has a radical conservative on its hands who puts not only Powell, but Chief Justice Warren E. Burger and Justice Harry A. Blackmun in the shade."[27]

Further evidence of the new justice's swashbuckling style of what some might see as radical activism occurred a few months later, when the American Civil Liberties Union asked Rehnquist to disqualify himself from a case and requested that the Supreme Court reconsider its 29 June 1972 decision on military surveillance, in which the sharply divided court had dismissed the ACLU's lawsuit on behalf of peace-group leaders and political dissenters on the grounds that it had failed to charge "specific" personal harm from the Defense Department's system of collecting dossiers on them and other civilians.[28] In a motion addressed directly to the justice, the ACLU said that "Justice Rehnquist's impartiality is clearly questionable" on the subject and that he had participated improperly in the 5-to-4 decision.[29] Despite his former role as the Justice Department's principal witness in Senate hearings on military spying when he was assistant attorney general, Rehnquist had joined the majority and had thus cast the deciding vote. Without his vote, the Court would have been evenly divided, which in this case would have resulted in a victory for the plaintiffs. At this juncture, questions about the judicial propriety of sitting on a case in which he had been previously involved appears not to have troubled Rehnquist in the least.

In 1986, however, he was quizzed about this and related matters once again during the Senate hearings on his nomination as Chief Justice. His evasive responses to the committee prompted a story entitled "Steel-Trap Mind, Sieve Memory," by syndicated columnist Paul Greenberg.[30] According to Greenberg, Rehnquist had explained a troubling discrepancy in his record concerning the army surveillance program after first telling the committee, "I had then and have no personal knowledge of the arrangement." After his disavowal, a Justice Department memo surfaced with his name on it, a memo that set out an arrangement for the army's surveillance of civilians. His explanation: "He can't remember having drafted such a plan," said Greenberg. That kind of explanation, Greenberg noted, "doesn't fit well with his admirers' portrait of William Hubbs Rehnquist as a brilliant advocate with a steel-trap mind. In this case, his memory resembles something closer to a steel sieve."

In Greenberg's opinion, Justice Rehnquist surely understood the significance of beginning such a surveillance program in a republic long concerned with separating military from civil concerns. The original plan itself, the one that bears his signature, speaks of "the salutary tradition of avoiding military intelligence activities in predominantly civilian matters." Yet his memo blurred the distinction between army and civilian intelligence agencies "to a dangerous degree, treating the Army as a useful tool against civil dissent," explained Greenberg.

The Rehnquist response to the committee in 1986 regarding this precedent-shattering arrangement was: "I have no recollection of my personal role in the preparation of this document. From the text of the transmittal memo I assume that the plan was primarily drafted by staff members in my office and in the office of the general counsel of the Army, and reviewed by me." Since "precedents are supposed to be a judge's forte," Greenberg observed, this raises some interesting questions about Mr. Rehnquist.

Rehnquist's responses reveal another quality of the justice that troubled the columnist: "The nominee does have a talent . . . for attributing the embarrassing to others—underlings, superiors, peers." In addition to shifting the blame to his subordinates and to the army in this case, Greenberg remembered Rehnquist's explanation of the controversial Justice Jackson memo on segregation, and this prompted him to conclude, "As scrutiny of this nomination continues—and it certainly should—it becomes clear that Rehnquist is blessed not only with a fine memory but, when suitable, a fine forgettery."[31]

At the same time as the ACLU petition was filed, lawyers for Senator Mike Gravel (D-Alaska), who also lost a 5-to-4 decision on 29 June 1972, filed a similar disqualification petition because of Justice Rehnquist's participation in their case.[32] They complained that Rehnquist had played a major part in the Pentagon papers controversy, which was involved in Gravel's case, before Rehnquist came to the Court.

Another 29 June 1972 decision by a 5-to-4 majority, with Rehnquist participating, stirred complaints that he had been a principal Nixon administration spokesman on the issue of grand jury subpoenas to newsmen. The case—which in-

volved Paul M. Branzburg of the *Louisville Courier-Journal,*
Earl Caldwell of the *New York Times,* and Paul Pappas of
television station WTEC-TV in New Bedford, Massachusetts—pitted the newspaper industry against the government's claimed power to subpoena unpublished and sometimes confidential information from newsmen. The *Post*
claimed to have learned, however, that none of the three
newsmen who had lost the decision would file rehearing peti-
tions.[33]

The paper pointed out that the rehearing motions by the
ACLU and Senator Gravel would probably not be considered
until the Court reconvened in the fall. Furthermore, it said,
such motions were rarely granted, because they require a
Court majority, which in these cases would include the vote
of at least one justice who had voted with the original majority. The majority in all three cases consisted of the four appointees of President Nixon—Burger, Blackmun, Powell, and
Rehnquist—plus White, a 1962 appointee of President Kennedy.

Cited as the authority for Rehnquist to recuse himself
from the cases were the latest draft of a proposed American
Bar Association code of judicial conduct and a federal law
requiring disqualification in any case in which a judge "has
substantial interest, has been of counsel, [or] is or has been a
material witness."[34]

The ACLU said Rehnquist had testified in Congress
about "the very lawsuit" that was before the justices and had
expressed the view that the suit should not be heard. Rehnquist was described by the ACLU as the administration's "expert witness" and the "custodian" of the Pentagon's top-se-
cret computer printout of army intelligence information on
civilian war-protest activities. Moreover, the former assistant
attorney general had also made several public speeches advo-
cating the Justice Department's position, the ACLU said. Indeed, Rehnquist's views were so well known, the petition
said, that the ACLU had been "convinced that Mr. Justice
Rehnquist would not participate and therefore had not
moved to disqualify him" at the outset of the case.[35]

111

Almost two months passed before Justice Rehnquist replied to the charges. On 10 September 1972 he denied that he had a conflict of interest in two of the cases decided in the last term and went further to insist that he had a duty to sit on both of them. He said it was both proper and legally required for him to sit on the cases that involved the army's surveillance of civilians and the Justice Department's attempt to question an aide to Senator Mike Gravel. As John P. MacKenzie, writing in the *Washington Post,* took pains to point out, such explanations are relatively rare.[36]

Under widespread attack by civil libertarians for casting crucial votes in the two decisions, Justice Rehnquist devoted a sixteen-page memorandum to the military surveillance case[37] but dismissed the Gravel case[38] with a footnote. In it he said that the ACLU had "seriously and responsibly urged" reasons for his disqualification in its petition for a new hearing by the other eight justices. Gravel's petition, on the other hand, he said, "possesses none of the characteristics" and did not require extensive answer. Indeed, he said that Gravel's petition "verges on the frivolous." He said his "peripheral advisory role" in the government's attempt to enjoin newpapers from publishing the Pentagon archives would have warranted his sitting out some cases but not the one involving Gravel, which was "a different case raising entirely different constitutional issues."[39]

In the army surveillance case, Rehnquist as assistant attorney general had testified that he believed the plaintiffs had failed to make a case of specific injury to their rights of privacy and free speech. That is exactly what the Supreme Court had held in handing down its 5-to-4 decision of 29 June 1972.[40]

Interestingly enough, Rehnquist's contention that he had a duty to sit on the case—that he would be letting the Court down if he disqualified himself in cases that were not clear-cut for recusing oneself—was the same argument he had made as a Justice Department official in support of Supreme Court nominee Clement F. Haynsworth, Jr. The Senate ultimately refused to confirm Haynsworth in 1969 after debate over whether he should have participated in certain cases on the Fourth United States Circuit Court of Appeals.[41]

In the surveillance case, Justice Rehnquist said he had not been either a counsel or a material witness. He went on to say that many judges throughout history have found and expressed opinions on "legal points" without disqualifying themselves later when the legal issue arose in their court. He did not, however, comment directly on the complaint that his public testimony related to the validity of the particular lawsuit that came before the Supreme Court, not merely the same legal issue.[42]

In summary, it can be seen that probably the most startling revelation to emerge from the 1971 hearings on the Rehnquist nomination to the Court was a memo he had written to Justice Jackson while he was his clerk in 1952 arguing that the 1896 separate-but-equal doctrine in *Plessy* v. *Ferguson* should be upheld. This was drafted a mere two years before the Court struck down the doctrine in *Brown* v. *Board of Education,* with Justice Jackson voting as part of the unanimous Court. Rehnquist's response in 1971, when the information surfaced, was to claim that the views expressed in the 1952 memo represented Justice Jackson's thinking, not his own.

The Rehnquist version, however, was sharply disputed by Jackson's longtime secretary, Elsie Douglas; University of Chicago law professor Philip Kurland, the custodian of the Jackson papers; and Jackson's biographer, Dennis J. Hutchinson, also of the University of Chicago. Hutchinson also found two more memos by Rehnquist indicating his views on race relations, one endorsing a lower-court ruling denying blacks the right to vote in Texas Democratic primary elections and the other attacking judicial efforts to strike down legally sanctioned segregation practices in the South.

The criticism of his race record, legal philosophy, and political ideology notwithstanding, the Senate in 1971 confirmed the nominee by a vote of 68 to 26, with little evidence that the criticism of Rehnquist during the hearing had won any converts. Indeed, some observers concluded that the debate had been counterproductive for his critics, since a number of the senators voting for his nomination clearly did not share his conservative views. Some senators were reluctant to use political ideology as the grounds for voting to reject because of its precedential impact in the future. Nonetheless, the only black member of the Senate at the time, Edward Brooke, was one of only three Republican senators to vote against Rehnquist's confirmation.

It became clear from the moment that Justice Rehnquist came to the Court that while he and Justice Powell might be conservatives, there was a vast difference between the traditional conservatism of Powell or of Chief Justice Burger, for example, and the more extreme variety reflected in the Rehnquist approach. This was probably more evident in their early years on the Court than it is in the 1980s, which may vindicate the views of Rehnquist critics who feared not only his vote but also his ability to alter the constitutional viewpoint of less forceful justices.

7

The End of the Beginning

AFTER the Sturm und Drang of the confirmation fight, Justice Rehnquist recalled thirteen years later, he soon came to recognize the uniqueness of his new position. "I can remember the day I moved over here [to the Court] from the Justice Department. I think it was three or four days before Christmas in 1971. . . . I brought my secretary and one of my special assistants from Justice who was going to be my law clerk."

"We came over here," he went on, "and it was a kind of gray afternoon, and everyone had left for Christmas. And I just felt, literally, like I'd entered a monastery when I came over. There was nobody around these long corridors, and there was some sort of an energy crises and only a couple of lights were on."

Then, becoming especially reflective, he mused, "Everybody who comes here probably feels the constraints of the place. I think the Court is remote."

"I have my own ways of trying to get away from the monasticism. I'm sure my colleagues have theirs. I visit law schools and make speeches and go to classes and have question and answer sessions. . . . I take a painting class at night school, where I mix with lots of people who are totally different from the kind of people I mix with regularly. And I'm thinking about maybe writing a book about the Court," he revealed.

Then in a remark suggestive of the fact that the old political activism still burns, he said, "You just have to keep anchors to the outside world, because a Justice of this Court does all of the work he has to do in the discharge of his oath of office without ever having to leave this building. The chambers are here, the courtroom is here, the library is here, the cafeteria is here. There's a gym and an exercise room. And, you know, it's just a two-dimensional world if you let that happen to you."[1]

The contention and acrimony of his confirmation hearings, which might have devastated some men, seemed to daunt Rehnquist very little, both at the time and in retrospect. For example, his office is adorned not only with portraits of Justices Robert H. Jackson and Oliver Wendell Holmes, and Chief Justices John Marshall and Charles Evans Hughes, but also a photograph of his former boss in the Nixon administration, John N. Mitchell, especially known for his role in the Watergate affair. Certainly the criticism leveled at him at the time of his appointment and immediately afterward did not prompt Rehnquist to pull into a shell or to play the game of judicial politics close to his vest.

As previously mentioned, he took the unprecedented action of refusing to recuse himself from several cases in which he had been involved while in the Justice Department. Indeed, he went further; in a subsequent action in which the ACLU brought suit seeking to force him to recuse himself from the *Tatum* case[2] and the *Gravel*[3] case, he not only sat on the case but made the definitive ruling in it. The answer to the ACLU's petition came on 10 October 1972, the first decision day of the new term. It read: "Motion to withdraw opinion of this Court denied. Motion to recuse . . . presented to Mr. Justice Rehnquist, by him denied." Next followed a sixteen-page memorandum from Justice Rehnquist that some observers consider to be as unusual for its contents as it was unprecedented.[4]

The ACLU's motion was based in part on the same federal disqualification statute that opponents of the Haynsworth nomination had cited in accusing him of impropriety.

116

It reads: "Any justice or judge of the United States shall disqualify himself in any case in which he has a substantial
interest, has been of counsel, or has been a material witness,
or is so related to or connected with any party or his attorney
as to render it improper, in his opinion, for him to sit.[5] Rehnquist, said the ACLU motion, had been a self-styled Justice
Department spokesman on the broad question of the constitutionality of the army surveillance of civilians (the alleged
illegality of which was at issue in the *Tatum* case), and had
appeared twice as a witness before Senator Ervin's subcommittee on constitutional rights, where he had argued that the
Pentagon surveillance program, however unwise or regretta-
ble, did not violate anyone's constitutional rights.[6] Further,
he also testified that the *Tatum* lawsuit, which was pending
in the lower courts while the Ervin hearings were under way,
was not, in his opinion, "justiciable" and that the courts
should and would dismiss the lawsuit for lack of standing.
(Interestingly enough, when the case came to the Supreme
Court, the Court, with Justice Rehnquist voting with the majority, ruled 5 to 4 that the issue was indeed nonjusticiable
and dismissed it for lack of standing.)[7]

In addition, Mr. Rehnquist in his prior role as a Justice
Department advocate had made clear to the Ervin committee
that the department was opposed to any legislative attempt
to control the military surveillance of civilians—which he
said had stopped anyway—or to impose a judicial remedy by
statute. The problem, he said, was best left to the self-discipline of the executive branch.[8]

The ACLU motion argued that Rehnquist had been an
advocate, not a mere spokesman, for the Justice Department
and that he had not limited himself to general statements
affirming the constitutionality of the program. Instead, said
the ACLU, "the concrete factual setting which he chose to
discuss was the surveillance of civilians by the United States
Army as depicted in the pleadings and the District Court decision in *Tatum* v. *Laird,* the very lawsuit" he later voted on
as a justice. Furthermore, the motion said, Rehnquist also
complied with a request from Senator Roman Hruska for a

legal memorandum supporting his constitutional thesis.[9] This Rehnquist memorandum denied that the program of surveillance had caused any interruption in vigorous public debate.

The ACLU motion also cited a decision disqualifying federal trial judge G. Harrold Carswell from a case that had been handled in his office when he had been a United States attorney.[10] The motion described it as "the interest any lawyer has in pushing his case to a successful conclusion." The ACLU thus attempted to define the term "case" broadly in order to suggest that the Ervin hearings and the *Tatum* lawsuit were parallel proceedings in different forums.

After citing this evidence in defense of its motion to reconsider, the ACLU concluded that "Justice Rehnquist's impartiality is clearly questionable because of his appearance as an expert witness for the Justice Department in Senate hearings inquiring into the subject matter of the case, because of his intimate knowledge of the evidence underlying the respondent's allegations, and because of his public statements about the lack of merit in the respondent's claims."[11]

Justice Rehnquist's response, in formally rejecting the ACLU motion, was first to interpret the American Bar Association's canons for disqualification and those of the federal statute as not "being materially different . . . [and thus] there is no occasion for me to give them separate consideration."[12] This startled a number of observers, because the new ABA canons were generally acknowledged to set a much stricter disqualification standard than those of the federal law. The ABA canons applied an "appearance of justice" test—which would disqualify a judge in doubtful cases—rather than the familiar "duty to sit" concept, which federal judges had developed to permit themselves to sit in doubtful cases. This approach was particularly interesting because Mr. Rehnquist had said at his confirmation hearings, that, if confirmed, he intended, when applying the federal disqualification law, "to try to follow that sort of stricter standards that I think the Senate, by its vote [in rejecting the Haynsworth appointment to the Supreme Court] indicated should prevail."[13]

In rejecting the ACLU motion the justice also argued that "I never participated, either of record or in any advisory capacity, in the District Court, in the Court of Appeals, or in this Court in the Government's conduct in the case of *Tatum* v. *Laird*." What he did by this statement was to reduce to its narrowest and most tortured meaning the word "case." With this definition he could, of course, argue that he had had no previous interest in the "case," nor had he participated in the "case."[14]

Finally, Rehnquist described the hazards he saw in an equally split vote on the Court. His withdrawal would have produced a 4-to-4 tie. He argued that a jurist has a "duty to sit" unless clearly disqualified, and he deemed it undesirable that a case heard by the Supreme Court should end in a tie— thus being "unsettled."[15] This approach may have some merit in a very general way, but it certainly was not valid in the *Tatum* case, where a tie vote would have sustained the court of appeals and thus required a trial on the merits of the dispute instead of avoiding the issues on jurisdictional grounds.

Nonetheless, Justice Rehnquist concluded his memorandum opinion in the second *Laird* case by noting:

> The oath prescribed by 28 U.S.C. Sec. 453 which is taken by each person upon becoming a member of the federal judiciary requires that he "administer justice without respect to persons, and do equal right to the poor and to the rich," that he "faithfully and impartially discharge and perform all the duties incumbent upon [him] . . . agreeably to the Constitution and laws of the United States." Every litigant is entitled to have his case heard by a judge mindful of this oath. But neither the oath, the disqualification statute, nor the practice of the former Justices of this Court guarantee a litigant that each judge will start off from dead center in his willingness or ability to reconcile the opposing arguments of counsel with his understanding of the Constitution and

the law. That being the case, it is not a ground for disqualification that a judge has prior to his nomination expressed his then understanding of the meaning of some
particular provision of the Constitution.[16]

In evaluating Mr. Rehnquist's behavior in this situation,
John MacKenzie wrote: "The sad conclusion—sad because it
must be made of a jurist with intellect, ability, and dedication
to the Court—is that Rehnquist's performance was one of the
most serious ethical lapses in the Court's history. Sad, too,
because his behavior, documented in his own extraordinary
memorandum justifying his conduct, came at an ethical watershed for the Court, when the distress of past scandals was
supposed to be behind us." Rehnquist's memorandum is the
only one ever published by a justice in response to a motion
to disqualify himself, a type of motion that is, of course, extremely rare. In MacKenzie's words, it is "a monument to
both Rehnquist's technical ability and his ethical short-
sightedness."[17]

Thirteen years later, in remembering his feelings at that
time, Rehnquist explained, "I came to the Court sensing,
without really having followed it terribly closely, that there
were some excesses in terms of constitutional adjudication
during the era of the so-called Warren Court." Then, in a mas-
terful understatement, he went on, "I felt that I probably
would disagree with some of those decisions." He explained
that while in private practice he had not paid a great deal of
attention to the ramifications of many of the key decisions of
the Warren Court. Nonetheless, he said, "the couple of cases I
did pay some attention to, seemed to me to be hard to justify
in terms of constitutional adjudication." Then, in summarizing his approach on assuming the bench, he observed, "I felt
that at the same time I came on the Court, the boat was kind
of heeling over in one direction. Interpreting my oath as I did,
I felt that my job was, where those sorts of situations arose, to
kind of lean the other way."[18]

Seeing this as his duty, what followed was a series of lone
dissents during his early years on the Court. In them, he
opposed school desegregation, women's rights, civil-service

jobs for aliens, and health care for the poor, among other inflammatory issues.[19] The inner gyrocompass of values that he brought to the Court continued firmly fixed, then as now. Because of these early solo dissents, his law clerks presented him in 1974 with a Lone Ranger doll, which can still be seen on the mantel of his office fireplace. "They referred to me as the 'lone dissenter,' " he chuckled in an interview.[20]

His critics, in reflecting on the values Rehnquist brought to the Court and the manner in which he consistently attempts to implement them, argue that he is, in fact, a judicial activist with a right-wing agenda. Justice Rehnquist, however, describes his philosophy and his legacy to the Court as "a sense of judicial restraint, for want of a better word." As he put it to John Jenkins, "We're carrying out a constitutional function that is a very delicate one. Every time we say that a law of Congress is unconstitutional, that a state law is unconstitutional, we are overriding a democratically reached decision. Now, the Constitution requires us to do that, but it requires us to do it only with great caution and circumspection." Because the Supreme Court is so "thoroughly undemocratic," said Justice Rehnquist, its role should be circumscribed. But, lest the listener lose perspective, he also pointed out that it is only a "little stream of history that flows by this Court, it's not a main channel at all." Reflecting on this point brought to his mind a literary quotation: "Who was it, Oliver Goldsmith, who said, 'How small, of all the ills that human hearts endure, that part that laws or kings can cause or cure'? " Yes, said Rehnquist, "I think that's just very, very true."[21]

Professor Owen Fiss of the Yale Law School and Charles Krauthammer of *The New Republic* see the Rehnquist approach quite differently. They acknowledge that Rehnquist's opinions are "clear, lucid, brief, and mercifully free of bureaucratese." Nonetheless, they observe, "his opinions fall radically short of the ideals of the profession." Rehnquist "repudiates precedents frequently and openly, and if that is impossible (because the precedent represents a tradition that neither the Court nor society is prepared to abandon), then he distorts them." As an example of this technique, Fiss and Krauthammer cite Rehnquist's handling of the *Debs* case, which involved one of the great labor strikes in American history. To Rehnquist this event was merely, as he wrote, "an armed conspiracy that threatened the interstate transportation of the mails."[22]

Furthermore, as Fiss and Krauthammer see it, Rehnquist "creates his own precedents out of asides: he places apparently inconsequential statements unobtrusively in one opinion, only to use them several opinions later—when he makes them seem of central importance to the earlier case and decisive to the case at hand." In addition, say Fiss and Krauthammer,

> He manipulates trial records, as when he tried to discredit the findings of a trial court, affirmed by a court of appeals, that a pattern of police harassment of minorities had occurred in Philadelphia. Rehnquist saw only isolated incidents. He will also occasionally substitute a slogan for analysis, as when he dismissed a grievance against overcrowded jails on the grounds that the Constitution does not guarantee "one man, one cell."[23]

Even such a relatively moderate journal as *Newsweek* took note, in its 30 June 1986 issue, of the fact that Rehnquist "sometimes even twists the facts." Moreover, *Newsweek* noted, "A [law] clerk once apologized for participating in writing a decision that Rehnquist refused to revise to reflect the true history of the federal welfare program".

Contrary to his hero's image among American conservatives, Rehnquist is not a conservative in the usual legal sense, nor does he believe in judicial self-restraint, which was the theme trumpeted by President Nixon when announcing his appointment and reiterated by President Reagan in June 1986 when announcing his elevation to chief justice. As Fiss and Krauthammer point out, he is instead a "revisionist," or "activist," of a "particular ideological bent." "He repudiates precedents," they say, "he shows no deference to the legislative branch; and he is unable to ground state autonomy," which is his guiding star, "in any textual provision of the Constitution." They also note that "when Rehnquist speaks of being guided by the 'tacit postulates' of the Constitution, he is referring neither to the needs of contemporary society nor to prevailing social morality—which he disparagingly calls 'the living Constitution.' " Instead, he wants the Court "to look back to 1787 and to reconstruct the intent of the drafters of the Constitution. [This is a theme echoed during the mid-1980s by Attorney General Edwin Meese.] The epistemological and evidentiary problems of such an undertaking are staggering."[24]

Moreover, this approach ignores the fact, as Professor H. Jefferson Powell of the University of Iowa Law School has pointed out in a series of most insightful articles, that the Founding Fathers, such as Madison, said they intentionally used certain vague words and phrases to permit later generations the opportunity to apply the document to contemporary economic and social problems they could not contemplate.[25] Madison explained this point in 1819 when he said: "It could not but happen, and was foreseen at the birth of the Constitution, that difficulties and difference of opinion might occasionally arise in expounding terms and phrases necessarily used in such a charter . . . and that it might require a regular course of practice to liquidate and settle the meaning of some of them."[26] Eleven years later Madison also spoke to this point in a letter to Martin Van Buren on 5 July 1830. He said, "For myself, I am aware that the document [the Constitution] must speak for itself, and that intentions cannot be substituted for [the intention as derived through] the established rules of interpretation."[27]

Justice Rehnquist takes his dedication to justifying state autonomy to the point, Fiss and Krauthammer believe, that he seems to confuse the Constitution with the Articles of Confederation. But the key problem with the Rehnquist approach, they say, is that it ignores the Civil War and the Civil War Amendments. The war decided the issue of state autonomy by denying the states the elemental facet of sovereignty—the right to withdraw from the Union. The Civil War Amendments codified this understanding, and they mark a second starting point in American constitutional law.[28]

The real thrust of the Rehnquist philosophy of state autonomy, as Fiss and Krauthammer demonstrate, is less to promote liberty than to promote property. In addition, it is used to repudiate the central value of the Warren Court—equality. The Warren Court's philosophy, as Fiss and Krauthammer see it—unlike the Rehnquist value system, which has remained consistent throughout—saw government power not as a necessary evil to be tolerated but as an important instrument for fully realizing the values embodied in the Constitution.[29]

In his 1985 interview with the *New York Times*, Rehnquist took a moment to compare the Burger Court to the Warren Court. He believed, he said, that the Burger Court's impact today has been diminished: "I don't think it has as wide a sense of mission. Perhaps it doesn't have any sense of mission at all."[30] He went on to make an important assessment of the role of the Court that some might see as being belied by his deeds while on the Court. He said, "I don't know that a court should really have a sense of mission. I think the sense of mission comes best from the President or the House of Representatives or the Senate. They're supposed to be the motive force in our Government. The Supreme Court and the federal judiciary are more the brakes that say, 'You're trying to do this, but you can't do it that way.' "

"The idea," he said, "that the Court should be way out in front saying, 'Look, this is the way the country ought to go,' I don't think was ever the purpose of the Court." Cases that do just that, such as *Brown, Miranda,* and *Roe* v. *Wade,* as Rehnquist evaluates them, are merely "exceptions that simply prove the rule."[31] It will be interesting to see whether this view prevails now that he is the chief justice.

His protestations against the Court having a sense of vision notwithstanding, the 1984 Republican party platform, which was firmly molded by the wing of that party to which Justice Rehnquist has been consistently tied, demanded a litmus test for future judicial appointments. The platform attacked the "elitist and unresponsive federal judiciary" and established a moral imperative for new federal judges: They must support "traditional family values" and oppose abortion.[32] "If the President thinks that an appointee ought to have particular views," Rehnquist told the *Times* interviewer, "I think that's the President's prerogative." "You know," he went on, "the Presidents who've tried to appoint people with a particular point of view," such as Lincoln and FDR, "have often only been partly successful because the judge is apt to sit long beyond the tenure of the President."[33]

Never one to be troubled by various judicial niceties, just three weeks before President Reagan's reelection the justice spoke at the University of Minnesota Law School. In his speech he downplayed the success any president can have in remaking the Court. This was widely seen by political analysts as an attempt to defuse an argument being made with some effectiveness by the Democrats that the great danger of a Reagan victory was that it would permit him to pack the Court with like-minded ideologues.[34]

"When a justice 'puts on the robe,' " he contended, "he puts aside partisanship." The theme was nothing new; it had surfaced nine years earlier. Nonetheless, as John Jenkins pointed out, "there was more than a little irony in Justice Rehnquist's preelection timing of his speech, and he inadvertently made the point he was trying to disprove: Even 13 years after his appointment, a Supreme Court Justice explicitly chosen for his doctrinaire conservatism was still a partisan, still sensitive to the political fray."[35]

There is no shortage of constitutional scholars who dispute the Rehnquist view of the limits of the president's effectiveness in influencing the direction of the Court through the appointive power. As Professor Tribe of the Harvard Law School wrote, "The President can strongly influence the direction of the Court, and the appointment of Justice Rehnquist is in itself an example of that." Looking at the altered composition of the Court in the years since Rehnquist's appointment in 1971, Tribe made a telling observation. "As he moves closer to the center as the Court moves right, his voice could become weaker against equally strong intellects." But as Tribe warned in this 1985 interview with John Jenkins, *"He could have an enormous impact, particularly if he were elevated to Chief Justice.* That has happened rarely because it causes terrible friction with the other Justices" (emphasis added).[36]

Also rejecting the Rehnquist version is Professor A. E. Dick Howard of the University of Virginia Law School. The Rehnquist thesis that presidents are often disappointed in their nominees loses its validity in the contemporary context, he believes.[37] Yet he is, nonetheless, impressed with Justice Rehnquist's influence on the Court. In a 1986 article published just before the announcement of Rehnquist's nomination as chief justice, Howard wrote that

> no justice of the Court generates more genuine warmth and regard among both his colleagues and others who work at the Court. A former law clerk to Justice White describes Rehnquist as "the nicest person at the Court. Within a few weeks of the Term's commencement, Justice Rehnquist knew all the clerks by their first names." A justice says of him, "Bill has an exceptional mind. No member of the Court carries more constitutional law in his head than he does." As one looks back over the nearly 15 years Rehnquist has been on the bench, the evidence mounts that he has become one of the most influential members of the Court. One of Rehnquist's colleagues suggests that one reason for Rehnquist's influence is the chief justice's inclination to assign him many of the important opinions.[38]

Since the fiasco associated with the nomination of Abe Fortas to be chief justice, Professor Tribe believes, "Congress and the White House have been much more sensitive to the ideology of a nominee."[39] In light of the June 1986 nomination of Judge Antonin Scalia to the Supreme Court, the re-

126

marks in 1985 by Professor Tribe are especially interesting as
he reacted to the Rehnquist thesis about obtaining a known
quality to the Court. "We're moving from a period where politics is no longer the name of the game, and ideology is what's
important in a judicial nominee. We're seeing this in the people that are mentioned most frequently as candidates for the
next Supreme Court vacancy: Robert H. Bork, and Antonin
Scalia. . . . They aren't politicians whose views might change
when they put on the robe. They are people who already have
very well-defined ideologies."[40]

"All these judges," said Yale Kamisar of the University of
Michigan Law School, "are former law school professors
(Bork taught at Yale and Scalia at Chicago) who are forceful
advocates of judicial restraint and laissez-faire government.
All were given appeals court judgeships by President Reagan
so he could have one last look." People like this, Kamisar
went on, "would be much less unpredictable than Supreme
Court nominees historically have been. They're established
conservative voices who've already demonstrated, as lower
court judges, how they'll decide certain cases."[41]

His many critics in academia have accused Justice Rehnquist of being disingenuous in his opinion writing. Fiss and
Krauthammer and others have noted his own perception of
the Constitution's "tacit postulates" or of a version of history
"too well known to warrant more than brief mention."[42] In
responding 'to this commonly heard accusation, Justice
Rehnquist told the *Times,* "If I thought it well founded in the
sense that I do things in a more disingenuous way than other
appellate judges, it would bother me." "But," he went on, "I
really don't to the extent I understand it. I don't think it is
well founded." As Justice Rehnquist saw it, "The suggestion
that I am disingenuous in going about the process of adjudication could be made equally well about my colleague Bill
Brennan. But I think there's a great deal more sympathy in
the law school faculties for the results he reaches than for the
results I reach."

He also saw his frequent role as a dissenter as contributing to confusion over his image. "In a dissenting opinion, that's really the purpose of a dissent: to lay the seeds for, hopefully, a change of doctrine."

Furthermore, he said of his academic critics, "they write somewhat disingenuously about me!" He pointed out that a poll of law-school faculty members during the 1972 presidential campaign showed 85 percent of them planned to vote for George McGovern in an election in which he carried one state. "You have to say that, based on the law of averages, the [typical law professor] author is going to start with something of a predisposition against a lot of my ideas. Because I do think that the political carries over some to the judicial philosophy," Justice Rehnquist concluded.[43]

In his prominent article in the December 1976 *Harvard Law Review,* Professor David Shapiro's assessment of Rehnquist's first four and a half years on the Court reverses the political point. He acknowledges that it is "unrealistic to expect that a newly appointed judge will come to the job without some established values and ideas, though they may well develop and change during the years on the bench. Indeed, the absence of values may lead to sterility and may minimize the judge's contributions to the work of the court."[44]

As noted earlier, it was Shapiro who, after studying Rehnquist's voting record for the first four and a half years, demonstrated that his votes are guided by three basic propositions:

>   1. Conflicts between an individual and the government should, whenever possible, be resolved against the individual;
>   2. Conflicts between state and federal authority, whether on an executive, legislative or judicial level, should, whenever possible, be resolved in favor of the states; and
>   3. Questions of the exercise of federal jurisdiction, whether on the district court, appellate court or Supreme Court level, should, whenever possible, be resolved against such exercise.[45]

The problem that troubles Shapiro about the Rehnquist approach is that "there should be sufficient flexibility to allow the development of a workable and coherent approach to the judicial function as well as the free exercise of intellectual capacity and full utilization of the lawyer's skills." In this respect, Shapiro concludes, "Justice Rehnquist has lacked that flexibility, and his judicial product has suffered as a result."[46] This point might well be kept in mind in light of Justice Rehnquist's recent appointment as chief justice in attempting to assess his effectiveness in giving a clearly conservative tilt to a Court that will bear his name.

In his 1986 article, A. E. Howard noted that "a review of Justice Rehnquist's opinions reveals that no one on the Court writes with more style, force or assurance. It is hard to match Rehnquist's agility in shaping a record and marshaling arguments to reach a conclusion."[47] He went on to identify certain themes that persist throughout the justice's opinions:

> Prominent among these is federalism—a belief that federal intervention into the affairs of a state requires convincing justification and ought to be the exception to the rule. Other themes include an adherence to the framers' original intent, a skepticism about judges setting out to solve social problems, a deference to legislative judgments and to the political process, and a belief that judicial review ought to be kept well within defined bounds.

This prompts Howard to conclude that "Justice Rehnquist has gone from being the 'lone dissenter' to being a key fighter in many of the major battles. Sometimes he wins, sometimes he loses. But when the history of the present Court is written, Justice Rehnquist will be recognized as a catalyst to many of that tribunal's great struggles."[48]

Justice Rehnquist seems relatively unbothered by newspaper editorials that have been sharply critical of him in the past. "They've bought the newspapers. They're entitled to express their views," he observed. Dealing particularly with the *New York Times* and the *Washington Post*, which have been consistently critical not only of his appointment but of the legal philosophy expressed in his written opinions, he pungently told his interviewer from the *New York Times,* "They have a particular point of view. If they want to be a house organ for the A.C.L.U., that's their privilege."[49]

In one area, nonetheless, press commentary did seem to nettle him. That was the coverage of his illness, for which he was hospitalized and which was brought on by his becoming addicted to the powerful pain-killing drug Placidyl, which had been prescribed for a chronic back problem. The media coverage, which described his slurred speech on the bench and the awkward slowness with which he sometimes spoke prior to hospitalization, bothered him "a little bit," he said in his interview with the *Times.* "But if you're bothered by what the press says about you, you're not cut out for this job," he concluded.[50]

Nonetheless, in the interview he would neither talk about the episode involving the pain-killing drug nor say much about his present state of health, except to remark testily: "I'm perfectly satisfied I can do my job. I suppose lots of unhealthy people are also perfectly satisfied they can do their jobs. But I'm going to stick by what I said." During the interview, however, his back prevented him from moving a coffee table, Jenkins pointed out. Yet he was also playing tennis once a week with his law clerks, which was a game he had to give up several years earlier because of his back problem.[51]

Some of Justice Rehnquist's remarks in his 1985 interview with the *Times* are noteworthy in light of the Reagan administration's professed interest in remaking the Court in its own image, and the recent appointment of Rehnquist as chief justice and Antonin Scalia as an associate justice. In the interview, Rehnquist said he saw virtue in diversity and would be loath to have eight colleagues who marched in lockstep with him. "Anything like a one-man or, I suppose in this day, a one-person Supreme Court would be an incredibly tyrannical thing," he remarked. "Obviously," he went on, "I don't have any clones around. As Bill Douglas used to say, 'The person I want appointed is someone who thinks just like me.' " Expanding on this point, he said, "You don't want eight of those people appointed, but, like all of my colleagues, I would welcome two or three people like me—I've been in dissent in a number of cases—perhaps some of those dissents would then become Court opinions. That's a very iffy business, though."

In 1985, despite the widespread speculation in the media about the likelihood of substantial turnover on the Court, Justice Rehnquist told his interviewer that he gave little thought to the prospect for change. "My nature is," he said, "I live one day at a time and don't look far into the future. I just kind of wrestle with what's at the front door now and don't worry a lot about what's going to show up tomorrow." Continuing on this theme, he said, "To live in the present means there's literally no time for thinking about past decisions: Was I right or was I wrong? You'd simply go nuts if you did that." Thus it should come as no surprise to learn, as he told the interviewer, that no opinion he has written stands out to him as being particularly noteworthy or memorable— "they're all kind of a long, gray line."[52]

Although they were poles apart ideologically, some observers speculated that there might be a similarity between Justice Douglas in his last decades on the Court and Justice Rehnquist during his first decade, in that they might both be iconoclasts. That is, if they were in lone dissent, they could say exactly what they wanted to say without worrying about getting other justices to agree with them in a majority opinion. Rehnquist, however, disputed this view. "I don't think of myself as being that way. I still think that one's major contribution comes by putting something together that commands a court opinion."[53]

Cathleen Douglas Stone, the widow of Justice Douglas and now a Boston lawyer, told the *New York Times* interviewer of the relationship between the two men soon after Justice Rehnquist came on the bench. Douglas "felt very sympathetic to Rehnquist, encouraged him to take up hobbies, and spent a lot of time with him, giving him the observations of Bill's own life and what it was like being a young man on the Supreme Court. When you come to the Supreme Court, the door closes. 'That has a different impact on a young man as opposed to, say, a man of 65.' Bill said, 'You can become a dry husk of a man.' "[54]

Reflecting on that point in 1985, Justice Rehnquist acknowledged that the position, "suits me better at age 60 than it did at 47." "At age 60," he said, "the life tenure looks good, and I know that if I were a senior partner in a law firm, with a nice corner office and views out both windows, a bunch of young people would be walking by wondering when I was going to go on semiretired status so they could have the office."[55]

Then, of considerable interest in light of his later appointment as chief justice on 17 June 1986, he spoke of retirement at age sixty-five. "I would love to get a new job when I am age 65 and could retire." "But," he went on, "those things just don't come along very often. I don't have any very good prospects except for staying here until I retire, and then probably doing a little teaching, or something like that."

Of course, those with overly cynical minds might speculate that one of the reasons he granted the unprecedented interview with the *Times* was to leak this bit of information to the Reagan administration—which, anxious as it was to keep his brand of legal activism on the Court, might be encouraged to seek ways of making his job there more appealing. Possibly, the offer of the chief justiceship would entice him to stay on the Court well beyond the permissible legal retirement age.

At the conclusion of the 1985 interview, Justice Rehnquist spoke on a subject that has regularly puzzled and intrigued Court-watchers and students of judicial behavior—his view on the necessary qualities and attitudes of a justice of the Supreme Court. "What qualities should a Supreme Court Justice possess," he mused. "what should a President look for?"[56]

"I think you have to be interested in the law, as kind of a discipline," Justice Rehnquist said. "I think you can be a successful lawyer without having any great interest in the

132

law. I'm not sure that you could be a successful appellate judge without having an interest in the law. I think you also have to enjoy writing," he went on. "And you have to enjoy analyzing things."

He then provided us with what may be one of the best insights into his personality: "But, over and above that, you have to be able to stand on your own two feet. I think it was Cicero who said about someone, 'He saw life clearly and he saw it whole.' " And, he went on, "You have to have a little bit of that in you." "Not being bamboozled by current, trendy ideas—that sort of thing. . . . It just captures something." "Not easily conned," he concluded, "Not awash in current trends of public opinion."[57]

Certainly, at this moment in our history, Justice William H. Rehnquist seems to meet these criteria if one sees with the eyes of an American conservative activist, to see life clearly and to see it whole.

If there is virtue in consistency, then Justice Rehnquist is indeed a virtuous man. On the other hand, it is worth remembering Ralph Waldo Emerson's observation, "A foolish consistency is the hobgoblin of little minds," and his trenchant comment, "With consistency a great soul has simply nothing to do." Of course, if there is a virtue in consistency, there is also no assurance that consistency will insure accuracy—accuracy in reading constitutional history or accuracy in reporting Court precedents. Nor does consistency guarantee a sense of what is fair and equitable, all of which are key elements in the concept of the due process of law. In short, consistency is no guarantee against wrongheadedness.

Notes

Preface

1. John A. Jenkins, "The Partisan: A Talk with Justice Rehnquist," *New York Times Magazine*, 3 March 1985, p.101.

1. Personal and Intellectual Origins

1. Fred Graham, "Nixon's Choices: Why He Apparently Made a Last-Minute Switch to Rehnquist," *New York Times*, 24 Oct. 1971.

2. James J. Kilpatrick, "Nixon Names Powell, Rehnquist," *Washington Post*, 22 Oct. 1971.

3. Ibid.

4. As quoted in *Time*, 1 Nov. 1971, p. 10.

5. Statements from the Rehnquist memo are taken from Mike Kurtz, "Rehnquist Argued ERA Would Harm the Family," *Washington Post*, 10 Sept. 1986.

6. "The Name Was Renchburg," *Washington Post*, 19 July 1974.

7. Clifton Fadiman, ed., *The Little, Brown Book of Anecdotes* (1985), p. 291.

8. "William H. Rehnquist," *Washington Post*, 22 Oct. 1971.

9. Ibid.

10. Ibid.

11. Spencer Rich, "Hill Reaction Is Favorable to Nominees," *Washington Post*, 22 Oct. 1971.

12. John P. MacKenzie, "Muskie Defends Security of Nominees," *Washington Post*, 25 Oct. 1971.

13. *Civil Liberties*, Jan. 1972, p. 8. This is a publication of the ACLU, which also sent a letter spelling out its opposition to the Rehnquist nomination to all members of the Senate.

14. Bayard Rustin, as quoted in the *New York Times*, 12 Dec. 1971; Andrew J. Biemiller, as quoted in the *Philadelphia Evening*

Bulletin, 10 Nov. 1971; Rev. George Benjamin Brooks, as quoted in the *New York Times,* 27 Nov. 1971.

15. *New York Times,* 17 Nov. 1971.

16. *Philadelphia Evening Bulletin,* 15 Nov. 1971.

17. *Washington Evening Star,* 15 Nov. 1971.

18. John A. Jenkins, "The Partisan: A Talk with Justice Rehnquist," *New York Times Magazine,* 3 March 1985, p. 31.

19. Ibid., p. 32.

20. Ibid., p. 32.

21. Ibid., p. 32.

22. David Shapiro, "Mr. Justice Rehnquist: A Preliminary View," *Harvard Law Review* 90 (1976): 293–357; Jenkins, "The Partisan," p. 31.

23. Owen Fiss and Charles Krauthammer, "The Rehnquist Court: A Return to the Antebellum Constitution," *The New Republic,* 10 March 1982, p. 16.

24. Ibid., p. 20.

25. Jenkins, "The Partisan," p. 31.

26. Ibid., p. 32.

27. Ibid., p. 32–33.

28. Ibid., p. 31.

2.   Political Theories and Labels

1. *New York Times,* 24 Oct. 1971.

2. Alan Dershowitz, "Of Justices and 'Philosophies,' " *New York Times,* 24 Oct. 1971.

3. *Washington Post,* 26 Oct. 1971.

4. Ibid. See also Shapiro, "Rehnquist: Preliminary View," 357.

5. *Washington Post,* 7 Nov. 1971.

6. See Tom Braden, "The Philosophy of William Rehnquist," *Washington Post,* 26 Oct. 1971.

7. Arthur S. Miller, "William Rehnquist: Legal Technocrat," *Washington Post,* 7 Oct. 1971.

8. Ibid.

9. *Washington Post,* 7 Nov. 1971.

10. Ibid.

11. Ibid.

12. Ibid., 5 Nov. 1971.

13. Ibid.

14. Ibid., 11 Nov. 1971.

15. Ibid.

16. For a discussion of the situation see Aaron Epstein, "Sen-

ate Foes Request FBI Probe of Rehnquist Role in Trust Fund," *Des Moines Register*, 27 Aug. 1986.

17. As quoted in the *Des Moines Register*, 27 Aug. 1986.

18. Ibid.

19. Miller, "William Rehnquist."

3. Media Views on the Rehnquist Philosophy

1. *Harvard Law Record*, 8 Oct. 1959.

2. "The Court Appointments," *New York Times*, 15 Oct. 1971.

3. *Harvard Law Record*, 8 Oct. 1959.

4. *New York Times*, 11 Nov. 1971.

5. Ibid.

6. Ibid., 15 Nov. 1971.

7. *Washington Post*, 9 Dec. 1971.

8. This refers to Rehnquist's article in the *Harvard Law Record*, 8 Oct. 1959, discussed earlier.

9. *Washington Post*, 10 Dec. 1971.

10. Ibid.

11. *National Review*, 19 Nov. 1971, p. 1283.

12. Ibid.

13. Ibid., 3 Dec. 1971, p. 1338.

14. Ibid.

15. Ibid., pp. 1338–39.

16. Ibid., p. 1339.

17. Ibid.

18. *Wall Street Journal*, 6 Dec. 1971.

19. *New York Times*, 15 Oct. 1971.

20. *National Review*, 19 Nov. 1971, p. 1283.

4. Mr. Justice Rehnquist and Civil Liberties

1. William Rehnquist, "The Notion of a Living Constitution," *Texas Law Review* 54 (1976): 693.

2. Charles Evans Hughes, *Addresses* (1908), p. 139.

3. Rehnquist, "Living Constitution," pp. 698–99.

4. Ibid., p. 699.

5. Ibid.

6. *Des Moines Register*, 20 Dec. 1984. This source also includes a further discussion of this issue.

7. Alexis de Tocqueville, *Democracy in America*, trans. Henry Reeve (1947), pp. 171–73.

8. Ibid., p. 171. For a detailed discussion of this point, see Tom

Braden, "The Philosophy of William Rehnquist," *Washington Post,* 26 Oct. 1971.

9. Spencer Rich, "Rehnquist's Civil Liberties Stance Eyed," *Washington Post,* 26 Oct. 1971. Rich's work includes a discussion of this and related views of Justice Rehnquist prior to his reaching the bench.

10. From a Law Day address on 1 May 1969, as quoted in *U.S. News and World Report,* 8 Nov. 1971, p. 44.

11. *Washington Post,* 7 Oct. 1971.

12. Ibid., 26 Oct. 1971.

13. As quoted in *U.S. News and World Report,* 8 Nov. 1971, pp. 43–44.

14. *New York University Law Review,* June 1970, as quoted in the *New York Times,* 11 Oct. 1971.

15. See Tom Braden, *Washington Post,* 26 Oct. 1971.

16. Presidential Appointments to the Supreme Court, University of Minnesota College of Law, Minneapolis, Minnesota, 19 Oct. 1984, mimeo, pp. 2–3.

17. Ibid., p. 23.

18. As noted in Rich, "Rehnquist Civil Liberties Stance."

19. From an address at the American Bar Association convention, London, 15 July 1971, as quoted in *U.S. News and World Report,* 8 Nov. 1971, pp. 42–43.

20. Rich, "Rehnquist Civil Liberties Stance."

21. From address before the Arizona Judicial Conference, Tempe, Arizona, 4 Dec. 1970, as quoted in *U.S. News and World Report,* 8 Nov. 1971, p. 44.

22. For a detailed discussion of these early views, see Rich, "Rehnquist Civil Liberties Stance."

23. Ibid.

24. *Washington Post,* 14 Feb. 1970.

25. *American Bar Association Journal,* March 1958, as quoted in the *New York Times,* 11 Nov. 1971. Joseph Rauh's testimony is also reported in the *Times* of this date.

26. *New York Times,* 11 Nov. 1971.

27. Ibid.

28. *Arizona University Law Review,* as reported in the *New York Times,* 11 Oct. 1971.

29. *Washington Post,* 22 Nov. 1971.

30. Ibid.

31. Ibid., 28 Nov. 1971.

32. Ibid., 1 Dec. 1971.

33. de Tocqueville, *Democracy,* p. 172.

34. *Washington Post,* 28 Nov. 1971.

5. Early Racial Views

1. *New York Times*, 28 Oct. 1971.
2. Ibid.
3. *Washington Post*, 30 Oct. 1971.
4. *New York Times*, 30 Oct. 1971.
5. Ibid.
6. *Washington Post*, 1 Nov. 1971.
7. Ibid.
8. Ibid., 30 Oct. 1971.
9. Senate Committee on the Judiciary, *Hearings on the Nomination of William H. Rehnquist*, 92d. Cong. 1st Sess., 3, 4, 8, 9, 10 Nov. 1971.
10. Ibid.
11. Ibid.
12. *Washington Post*, 4 Nov. 1971.
13. Ibid.
14. Ibid.
15. Ibid.
16. Ibid., 10 Nov. 1971.
17. *Time*, 11 Aug. 1971, p. 14.
18. Ibid.
19. Ibid.
20. Ibid.
21. Ibid.
22. Ibid., 18 Aug. 1986, p. 23.
23. Ibid., 11 Aug. 1986, p. 14.
24. *Washington Post*, 13 Nov. 1971.
25. Ibid.
26. Ibid., 3 Dec. 1971.
27. *Washington Post*, 4 Dec. 1971.
28. *Arizona Law Review*, Summer 1970, as quoted in the *New York Times*, 11 Nov. 1971.
29. The text of the two memorandums was printed in the *New York Times*, 17 March 1972.
30. Senate Committee, *Hearings.*
31. *Time*, 11 Aug. 1971, p. 14.
32. Ibid.; *Time*, 18 Aug. 1971, p. 23.

6. More Controversy over Race, Theory, and Procedure

1. As quoted in Owen Fiss and Charles Krauthammer, "The Rehnquist Court," *The New Republic*, 10 March 1982, pp. 14–15.
2. *Washington Post*, 6 Dec. 1971.

3. Ibid. 11 Dec. 1971.
4. Ibid., 9 Dec. 1971.
5. Ibid.
6. Ibid., 10 Dec. 1971.
7. Ibid.
8. Ibid., 11 Dec. 1971.
9. Ibid.
10. Ibid.
11. John A. Jenkins, "The Partisan: A Talk with Justice Rehnquist," *New York Times Magazine*, 3 March 1985, p. 32.
12. Ibid., p. 32.
13. Ibid., p. 32.
14. *Washington Post*, 10 Dec. 1971.
15. Ibid.
16. Ibid.
17. Ibid., 11 Dec. 1971.
18. Ibid.
19. Ibid., 26 Dec. 1971.
20. Ibid.
21. Ibid.
22. Ibid.
23. John P. MacKenzie, "The Rehnquist-Powell Split," *Washington Post*, 13 May 1972.
24. *Weber* v. *Aetna Casualty & Surety*, 92 Supreme Court Reporter 1400 (1972) (hereafter cited as S.Ct.); MacKenzie, "The Rehnquist-Powell Split."
25. *Cruz* v. *Beto*, 92 S.Ct. 1079 (1972); MacKenzie, "The Rehnquist-Powell Split."
26. MacKenzie, "The Rehnquist-Powell Split."
27. Ibid.
28. *Laird* v. *Tatum*, 92 S.Ct. 2318 (1972).
29. *Washington Post*, 19 July 1972.
30. *Des Moines Register*, 3 Sept. 1986.
31. Ibid.
32. *U.S.* v. *Gravel*, 92 S.Ct. 2614 (1972).
33. See *Branzenburg* v. *Hayes*, 92 S.Ct. 2446 (1972); *U.S.* v. *Caldwell*, 92 S.Ct. 2646 (1972); *U.S.* v. *Caldwell*, 92 S.Ct. 2686 (1972); *Washington Post*, 19 July 1972.
34. *Washington Post*, 19 July 1972.
35. Ibid.
36. Ibid., 11 Sept. 1972.
37. *Laird* v. *Tatum*.
38. *U.S.* v. *Gravel*.
39. *Laird* v. *Tatum*, 93 S.Ct. 7 (1972).
40. *Laird* v. *Tatum*, 92 S.Ct. 2318 (1972).

41. *Washington Post,* 11 Oct. 1972.

42. *Laird* v. *Tatum,* 93 S.Ct. 7 (1972).

7. *The End of the Beginning*

1. John A. Jenkins, "The Partisan: A Talk with Justice Rehnquist," *New York Times Magazine,* 3 March 1985, p. 100.

2. *Laird* v. *Tatum,* 92 S.Ct. 2318 (1972).

3. *U.S.* v. *Gravel,* 92 S.Ct. 2614 (1972).

4. *Laird* v. *Tatum,* 93 S.Ct. 7 (1973).

5. 28 United States Code Annotated, sec. 455.

6. John P. MacKenzie, "The Rehnquist Recuse: Judging Your Own Case," *Washington Monthly,* May 1974, p. 54.

7. Ibid.; 92 S.Ct. 2318 (1972).

8. MacKenzie, "The Rehnquist Recuse," p. 57.

9. 93 S.Ct. 10–11.

10. See Nomination of Clement F. Haynsworth, Jr., Executive Report No. 91-92, 91st Cong. 1st Sess., pp. 10–11.

11. 93 S.Ct. 9.

12. Ibid.

13. MacKenzie, "The Rehnquist Recuse," p. 59.

14. 93 S.Ct. 10–11.

15. Ibid., pp. 15–16.

16. Ibid., p. 15.

17. MacKenzie, "The Rehnquist Recuse," p. 54.

18. Jenkins, "The Partisan," p. 33.

19. *Columbus Board of Education* v. *Penick,* 443 *U.S. Reports* 449 (1979) (hereafter cited as U.S.); *Craig* v. *Boren,* 429 U.S. 190 (1976); *Sugarman* v. *Dougal,* 413 U.S. 634 (1973); *New Jersey Welfare Rights Organization* v. *Cahill,* 411 U.S. 619, 621 (1973).

20. Jenkins, "The Partisan," p. 34.

21. Ibid., p. 88.

22. Owen Fiss and Charles Krauthammer, "The Rehnquist Court," *The New Republic,* 10 March 1982, pp. 15–16.

23. Ibid., p. 16.

24. Ibid., p. 20.

25. See, for example, H. Jefferson Powell, "The Original Understanding of Original Intent," *Harvard Law Review* 98 (1985): 885–948; H. Jefferson Powell, "The Constitution's Framers' Intent Irrelevant," *Des Moines Register,* 28 Jan. 1986.

26. As quoted in Powell, "Framers' Intent."

27. As quoted in Powell, "Original Understanding," p. 936.

28. Fiss and Krauthammer, "The Rehnquist Court," p. 20.

29. Ibid., p. 21.

30. Jenkins, "The Partisan," p. 35.

31. Ibid.
32. Ibid.
33. Ibid., pp. 35, 88.
34. Ibid., p. 88.
35. Ibid.
36. Ibid., pp. 88, 31.
37. Ibid., p. 88.
38. A. E. Howard, "Justice Rehnquist—A Key Fighter in Major Battles," *ABA Journal,* 15 June 1986, p. 47.
39. Jenkins, "The Partisan," p. 88.
40. Ibid.
41. These views are found in Jenkins "The Partisan," p. 88.
42. Fiss and Krauthammer, "The Rehnquist Court," p. 20.
43. Jenkins, "The Partisan," p. 34.
44. David Shapiro, "Mr. Justice Rehnquist: A Preliminary View," *Harvard Law Review* 90 (1976): 294.
45. Ibid.
46. Ibid., p. 357.
47. Howard, "Justice Rehnquist," p. 49.
48. Ibid.
49. Jenkins, "The Partisan," p. 101.
50. Ibid.
51. Ibid., p. 101.
52. Ibid., pp. 88, 100.
53. Ibid., p. 101.
54. Ibid.
55. Ibid.
56. Ibid.
57. Ibid.

Index

ABA (American Bar Association),
  3–5, 45, 94, 111, 118
ABA Committee on the Federal
  Judiciary, 3–5, 79–82
Academic critics, 127–28
Acheson, Dean, 27
Activist, 49, 56, 122, 133
Adams, John, 24
Aetna Casualty and Surety
  Company, 107
American Bar Association (ABA),
  3–5, 45, 94, 111, 118
American Civil Liberties Union, 11–
  12, 116–19
Americans for Democratic Action,
  39, 78
Antibusing legislation, 91. *See also*
  Busing
Apparatchik, 26
"Appearance of justice" test, 118
Arizona Bar Association, 76, 78
Arizona Law Review, 90
Arizona legislature, 75
"Arizona Mafia," 38
Arizona Republic, 76–77, 89
Arizona State University College of
  Law, 83
Army surveillance case, 109–10,
  112
Articles of Confederation, 123
Associated Press, 7
Attorney general, 68, 89

Baker, Russell, 80–81
Ballot security, 90
Bartley, Robert L., 52–54
Bayh, Birch, 29–30, 38, 68, 73, 85,
  94, 99, 100, 104, 108
Berg, Richard K., 69–70
Best and the Brightest, The, 81
Bill of Rights, 15, 36, 51–54, 70,
  71, 74
Black, Charles L., 42
Black, Hugo, 3, 8, 25, 84
Blackmun, Harry A., 3, 8, 17, 106,
  108, 111
Black separatists, 88
"Blockbusting," 68
Boldt, Judge, 30–32
Bork, Robert H., 83, 127
Braden, Tom, 24
Brandeis, Louis, 21, 42
Brooke, Edward W., 88–89, 104–5,
  114
Brooks, Rev. George B., 75–76
Brosnahan, James, 87
Brown v. *Board of Education*, 50,
  78, 97–98, 102, 113, 124
Brzezinski, Zbigniew, 26
Bugging, electronic, 36, 48
Burger, Warren, 8, 17, 39, 106, 108,
  111, 114
Burger Court v. Warren Court, 124
Busing, 85–94, 96

Cabinet departments, 68
Cambodia, 60
Campbell, Cloves, 75
Carswell, Harrold G., 3, 9, 17, 39–
    40, 49, 61, 65, 105, 118
Case, Clifford P., 105
Case, Definition of, 118–19
"Case or controversy," 117–18
Caucasian race, 88, 96
Character assassination, 88
Chief Justice, 6, 8, 32, 80, 86, 109,
    122, 124, 126
Civil disobedience, 23
Civil dissent, 110
Civil liberties, ix, 42, 55, 57, 66–67,
    71–72, 74, 88, 98, 106
Civil rights, 65, 67, 70–71, 73–74,
    82
Civilian intelligence agencies, 110
Civil War amendments, 15, 123–24
Clawson, Ken W., 9–10
"Closeup," ABC documentary, 55
Coke, Lord, 28
Commager, Henry Steele, 27
Commissioners on Uniform State
    Law, transcript of meeting, 68
Committee on the Federal
    Judiciary, ABA, 3–5, 79–82
Communists, 65–66, 71, 74
Confirmation hearings, ix, 11, 19,
    22, 28, 30, 32, 37–38, 68, 84–
    88, 99, 116, 118
Congress, 23, 31, 44, 56, 65, 94,
    101, 104, 121, 126
Conservative, 5, 11, 15, 18, 20, 24,
    33, 36, 42, 57, 82, 84, 114, 133
Constitution, 5, 8, 14, 15, 20, 23,
    29, 36, 46, 49, 55–56, 90, 92,
    103, 106, 107, 119, 123, 124
  color blind, 53
  framers of, 51
  living, 55, 123
  tacit postulates of, 16, 123, 127
Constitutional adjudication, 120
Constitutional amendment, barring
    busing, 91, 96
Constitutional democracy, 36
Constitutional Rights Subcom-
    mittee, Senate, 59, 64, 117
Cornell, Harold D., 33

Corwin, Edward, 26
Court. See Supreme Court
Court-packing, 61–63, 125
Cranston, Alan, 32
Criminal law, 45, 106
Criminal procedure, 64
Criminals, protection against, 8
Critics, academic, 127–28
Cronson, Donald, 100–101

Declaration of war, 59–60
De facto segregration, 38, 77, 92
De jure segregation, 90
Democracy in America, 57
Demonstrations, public, 58–59
Dershowitz, Alan, 21–22
Des Moines Register, 7–8
Disqualification
  canons of American Bar
    Association, 118–19
  federal statute, 111, 116–18
Domestic tranquility, 51, 54
Douglas, Elsie, 102–3, 113
Douglas, William O., 131–32
Dual school systems, 85
Due process, 16, 23, 51, 64, 133
"Duty to sit" test, 118

Eastland, James O., 11, 30, 80,
    98–99
Ehrlichman, John, 9
Eisenhower, Dwight D., 4, 105
Electronic surveillance, 23, 36, 59
Elite values, 44
Emerson, Ralph Waldo, 81, 133
Equal Protection Clause, 51, 107
Equal Rights Amendment (ERA),
    5–7
Ervin, Sam, 27, 59, 117
Evidence, illegally seized, 57
Exclusionary rule, 64
Executive appoinHve authority, 61,
    62, 68
Executive branch, 23, 24, 36, 48,
    59, 68, 70, 104, 117

Executive privilege, 27, 65
Expert witness, 111, 118
Extremist, 24, 34

Fannin, Paul, 84
FBI, 32, 33, 87
First Amendment, 11, 25, 27, 43, 51
Fiss, Owen, 15, 121-24, 129
Flag salute, compulsory, 104
Fortas, Abe, 40, 126
Founding fathers, 36, 56, 123
Frank, John P., 77-78
Frankfurter, Felix, 22, 28, 41, 102
Freedom of choice, 76, 91, 92
Free speech, 25, 51, 71, 73, 74, 112
Friday, Herschel H., 4, 17
Fulbright, William, 104

Garment, Leonard, 5
George Washington University, 25
Goldberg, Arthur, 47
Goldwater, Barry, 12, 38, 45, 77
Governmental authority, ix, 64, 73, 74
Graham, Fred P., 22-23
Grand jury subpoenas to newsman, 110
Gravel, Mike, 110-12
Greenberg, Paul, 109
Gurney, Edward, 27

Halberstam, David, 81
Hand, Learned, 41-43
Harding, Warren G., 72
Harlan, John M., 3, 4, 8, 22, 29, 66
Harlbut, John B., 83
Hart, Gary, 73
Harvard Law Record, 23, 35, 53-54
Harvard Law Review, 14-15
Haynsworth, Clement, 3, 17, 39, 40, 50, 105, 112, 116
Herblock, 43, 45-47

Hebrew race, anti-Semitism, 87-88, 95-96
Holmes, Oliver Wendell, 21, 27, 28, 34, 43, 105, 116
Howard, A. E. Dick, 126, 129
Hruska, Roman, 9, 30, 32, 117
Hughes, Charles Evans, 23, 56, 116
Huntington, Samuel, 26
Hutchinson, Dennis J., 103, 113

Ideological issues, 9, 12, 18, 41, 50, 114, 122, 127
Illiteracy and right to vote, 86
Individual rights, ix, 48, 64-65, 71-74
Invasion of privacy, 48
Investigative authority, 48, 57, 59, 63, 64, 72

Jackson, Robert, 14, 97-98, 100-104, 110, 113
Javits, Jacob K., 104, 105
Jefferson, Thomas, 24
Jehovah's Witnesses, 104
Jenkins, John A., 12, 16
Jenner, Albert, Jr., 69
John Birch Society, 66, 75, 76, 88
Johnson, Lyndon, 40
Judicial activist, 15, 22, 24, 38, 121
Judicial branch of government, 56, 61
Judicial conservative, 8, 15, 20, 24, 34, 38
Judicial decision-making, x, 17, 22, 105
Judicial disqualification, 111, 116-19
Judicial function, limits on, 41-43, 97, 122
Judicial nominating process, 3-5
Judicial philosophy, 11, 20-23, 29-30, 34, 128
Judicial politics, 116
Judiciary Committee, Senate, 11, 22, 28, 32, 65, 66, 76, 83, 84, 85, 98, 108

Justice Department, 5, 9, 10, 29, 32, 64, 65–69, 73, 76, 77, 83, 84, 91, 109, 111, 115–118

Kamisar, Yale, 127
Kaplan, Jarril F., 83
Kauper, Thomas E., 83
Kennedy, Edward, 29, 32, 38, 39, 40, 45, 52, 67, 73, 81, 88, 111
Kilpatrick, James J., 12
King, Martin Luther, 71
Kleindienst, Richard G., 17
Kraft, Joseph, 43–47
Kurland, Philip B., 101–2, 113

Laird v. *Tatum*, 116–19
Law-and-order philosophy, 5, 21, 37, 77
Law Day Address, Newark, Del., 58
Lawyer-client relationship, 29, 37, 53
Lawyers, 9, 57, 73
Leadership Conference on Civil Rights, 65–67, 76, 85, 88
Legal Defense Fund, 7
Legality, 57, 69, 73
Lewis, Anthony, 41–42
Lewis, Flora, 47
Liberal, 18, 20, 24, 36, 107
Lichtman, Judith, 7
Lillie, Mildred L., 4, 17
"Limited martial law," 58
Lincoln, Abraham, 62, 125
Lindsay, John V., 11
Literacy tests, oral, 89–90

McCloskey, Paul N., Jr., 11
McGovern, George, 128
MacKenzie, John P., 107, 108, 120
McReynolds, James R., 22, 42, 106
Madison, James, 123
Maggiore, Victor, 87
Mann, Judy, 7
Marshall, Thurgood, Justice, 98

Material witnesses, iii, 113, 117
Mathias, Charles, 105
Media, 35, 48, 54, 90, 94, 130, 131
Metzenbaum, Howard, 32
Middle-of-the-roaders, 45, 47
Military surveillance, 109–13, 117
Miller, Arthur S., 25, 26, 28, 70
Mills, Billie, 75
"Minnesota Twins," 106
Minorities, 46, 47, 57, 71, 84, 85, 122
Miranda case, 43, 124
Mitchell, Clarence, 89–90
Mitchell, John N., 3–5, 30, 37, 45, 67, 76, 88, 105, 106, 116
Model civil rights act, 69
Multi-racial school districts, 93
Muskie, Edmund, 11

NAACP
  Arizona, 75
  Phoenix, 75
  Virginia Conference, 77
National Organization for Women, 7
National Review, 49–51, 54
National security, 64
Neal, Phil C., 83–84
Negroes, in Arizona, 88–90
Neighborhood school issue, 77, 85, 92–94
"Neo-realist judicial philosphy," 42
"New barbarians," 58–59
New Right, 25, 57
Newsweek, 97, 98, 122
New York City Bar Association, 59
New York Times, 12, 22, 33, 35, 39, 41, 53, 75, 80, 91, 103, 111, 124, 129, 130, 131
New York University, 57
New York University Law Review, 60
Nixon, Richard, 3, 4, 5, 8, 9, 10, 17, 19, 20, 22, 25, 26, 29, 30, 34, 35, 37, 40, 45, 47, 48, 50, 53, 55, 60, 63, 67, 72, 74, 94, 100, 105, 106, 108, 122
  and Pay Board, 31
  and selection of Supreme Court

146

candidates, 3–5, 35
"No knock" raids, 52–53

O'Connor, Sandra, 84
Office of Legal Counsel, 5, 17, 26,
69–70

Parker, Isaac C., 16
Pentagon papers controversy, 110
Philadelphia, 10, 68, 69, 122
Phillips, Kevin, 12
Phoenix City Council, 76
Phoenix Human Relations
Commission, 83
Plessy v. *Ferguson*, 97–99, 101,
113
Police harassment, 122
"Police sweeps," 58
Political philosophy, 16, 19, 38, 66
Populist country, 44
Pornographers, 49, 54, 71, 74
Powell, H. Jefferson, 123
Powell, Lewis, 4, 8, 9, 36, 38, 39,
105, 107, 108, 111, 114
Precedents, judicial, 21, 38, 110,
122–23
President
as commander in chief, 59–61
and judicial appointments, 35–
36, 41, 61–63, 95, 125–26
Pretrial detention, 64
Preventive detention, 36, 52, 57
Privacy
invasion of, 48
right to, 36, 71
Probable cause, 63
Property rights, 71, 85, 98, 124
Protest, peaceful, 71, 74
Proxmire, William, 104, 105
Public accommodation law
national, 71, 85–86
in Phoenix, 94

Racial balance, in schools, 90–92,
96

Racial equality, 68, 73
Radical activism, 108
Rauh, Joseph, 39, 40, 65, 78, 85,
89–90
Reagan, Ronald, 19, 44, 61, 122,
125
Recidivists, 64
Recuse, 111, 116–17
Rehearing motions, 111
Rehnquist, William H.
ACLU motion to recuse, 110–13,
116–17
appointment to Court, 4–5
as assistant attorney general, 25–
26, 29, 63–65
black voters, actions toward, 86–
87
busing, writings on, 85–94
Cambodia, invasion of, 60
childhood, and family
background, 12–13
civil disobedience, 23
civil liberties, attitude toward,
36–37, 57–59, 72, 82
civil rights, attitudes toward, 69–
71, 73–75, 82
clerkship, 14, 97–98, 113
conservative activism, 16–18
consistency of views, ix, 34, 70,
80–81, 132–33
constitution, philosophy
regarding, 55–57, 106, 121
court-packing, views on, 61–63,
125
demonstrators, reaction to, 58–59
disingenuous opinions, 129
education, college and graduate,
13–14
ERA, attitudes toward, 5–8
extremist, viewed as, 19, 24, 34
FBI investigation, 32–33
Fourteenth Amendment, views
on, 107–8
government wiretapping, 64
health problems of, 139
housing restrictions, anti-Semitic,
87–88, 95–96
iconoclast, 131
illegitimate children, views on,
107–8

147

Rehnquist, William H. (*continued*)
as judicial activist, 15, 24, 121
as judicial conservative, 15, 20, 22, 24, 122–24
judicial philosophy, 17–18, 20–21, 29
judicial temperament, 27
justice, guided by basics, 11, 128
Law Day address, 58
law practice of, in Phoenix, 16
legislative branch, reactions from, 11–12
lone dissents, 120–21, 128, 129
McCarthyite accusation, 65, 78
memorandum, on segregation, 97–101
memorandum, *Laird* Case, 119–20
misconduct charges, 30–34
National Review, views on, 49–51
Newark Kiwanis club speech, 23
New York Times, views on, 35–40, 53, 130
as Nixon appointment, 9, 20
in Office of Legal Counsel, 19, 26, 69
origins, intellectual and personal, 12–18
partisan, opinion on, 14
Philadelphia plan, 10
philosophy toward Court, 121
and pluralism, 16
as political conservative, 10, 22, 33–34
President's effectiveness, views on, 125
qualifications, professional and intellectual, 20, 24, 26, 45–46, 77–83
race relations, views on, 68, 84–86, 103–4
racial views, early, 75–76
racist, labeled as, 82–83
reactionary, viewed as, 28
and Republican platform, 1984, 124
reminiscences of, 115, 120, 124, 131–33
revisionist, viewed as, 122

school segregation, views on, 76–77
Senate confirmation hearings of, iii, 11, 19, 28–32, 37–38, 95–96, 104–5
separate but equal doctrine, views on, 97–104, 109
speeches, public, 23, 38
stare decisis, views on, 14, 23, 107
state autonomy, views on, 10, 15–16, 123–24
strict constructionist, viewed as, 25
subpoena to newsman, views on, 110–11
Subversive Activities Control Board, views on, 27
surveillance, and courts, 23, 59, 108–10, 112–13
trust fund, investigation of, 32–33
voter intimidation, of Blacks and Hispanics, 86–87, 95
Wall Street Journal, views of, 52–53
Washington Post, views of, 47–48, 71, 130
women, attitudes toward, 5–8
Religious privilege, prison, 108
Republican party platform, 1984, on judicial appointments, 124–25
Retirement, of Rehnquist, 132
Right wing, x, 11, 18, 34, 38, 41, 45, 66, 88, 121
Roe v. *Wade*, 124
Roosevelt, Franklin, 20, 48, 62
Roosevelt, Theodore, 28, 105
Roosevelt Court, The, 20

Saxbe, William, 61
Scalia, Antonin, x, 126, 127, 130
School boards, and neighborhood school issue, 92–94
Search
and seizure, 66
of prisoners, 57, 63, 72

unreasonable, 63
vehicles, 59
Self-discipline, 36, 117
Senate, 4, 5, 36, 45, 49, 58, 70, 76, 86, 124
Senate, Constitutional Rights Subcommittee, 59, 64, 117
Separate but equal doctrine, 97–104, 113
Sexton, John, 57
Shannon, William V., 37, 53
Shelly v. *Kramer*, 87
Slaughterhouse Cases, 108
Smeal, Eleanor, 7
Smith, Sidney, 86
Social activists, 49
Solicitor general, 102
"Speedy trial" bill, 29
Spying, 29, 109
Standing, doctrine of, 117, 128
Stanford Law School, 11–24, 79, 83
Stare decisis, 14, 22–23, 107
State autonomy, 15, 123–24
Steinem, Gloria, 7
Stevenson, Adlai E., 105
Stone, Cathleen Douglas, 131
Stream of history, 121
Strict constructionist, 25, 45, 49
Subcommittee on Separation of Powers, 25, 26–27
Subversive Activities Control Board, 27, 65
Supreme Court, x, 100, 105. *See also* Rehnquist, William H.
   ethical watershed, 120
   tie notes, 119
Surveillance, 23, 72, 109–113, 117
Switzerland, Gstaad, 101

Taft, William Howard, 72
Terry v. *Adams*, 103–4
Texas Democratic Club, 103
Texas Law Review, 55–56
Thurmond, Strom, 32
Time, 16, 37, 86, 91, 95, 125, 127, 130
Tocqueville, Alexis de, 57–58, 73
Tribe, L., 125–27
Tunney, John, 73

University of Chicago Law School, 83, 101
University of Iowa Law School, 123
University of Michigan Law School, 83, 127
University of Minnesota College of Law, 61, 125
University of Virginia Law School, 126
U.S. Court of Appeals, Fourth Circuit, 113

Van Buren, Martin, 123
von Dreele, W. H., 49
Voters
   Black, 86, 87, 88, 95
   Hispanic, 86, 87, 95

Wall Street Journal, 52, 54
War protest activities, Pentagon response, 111
War protesters, 23, 49, 58
Warren, Earl, 22, 34, 44, 106
Warren Court, 42, 43, 46, 47, 49, 55, 65, 120, 124
Washington Post, 7–9, 30, 31, 43–48, 49, 65, 69–72, 77, 89, 100, 101, 102, 105, 112, 129
Wedlock, 6, 107
Welfare program, federal, 162
White, Byron, 24, 111, 126
White separatists, 88
Wicker, Tom, 39–40
Wilkins, Roy, 77
Wilson, Woodrow, 105
Winter, Ralph K., Jr., 83
Wiretapping, 29, 36, 64–65, 73

Yale Law School, 15, 83, 121

Ziegler, Ronald L., 4–5